THE WAY WE WERE

DECLAN HASSETT

MERCIER PRESS

MERCIER PRESS
5 French Church Street, Cork
16 Hume Street, Dublin 2

Trade enquiries to CMD DISTRIBUTION,
55a Spruce Avenue, Stillorgan Industrial Park, Blackrock, Dublin

© Declan Hassett, 1999

ISBN 1 85635 288 9

10 9 8 7 6 5 4 3 2 1

FOR MY CHILDREN
AND GRAND-CHILDREN

Printed in Ireland by ColourBooks Ltd.

CONTENTS

THE LOST TEARS

People meet, embrace at airports, they laugh and I cry. A brass band parades down a summer street, everyone smiles, I cry. Yet, I never cried when my father and mother died. Those whom I love deeply depart this world and I am not moved to tears. I can crumble at a line from a song, disintegrate when Bogart eyes Bergman and then walks away into the fog. I worry about this seeming indifference to moments of genuine tragedy and then collapse at the trivial.

I did cry when Orla died. She would be thirty now if she had lived; a delicate child from birth, we lost our daughter through illness when she was just ten months old but she has never really left us.

Orla died on the anniversary of our wedding day, so each year we make less of the memory of that great day now thirty-five years ago. The well intentioned assume that the sense of loss, the sense of helplessness does ease with the years, and to be honest, it helps, but little things can reopen the wound and there is no pain-killer strong enough to dull the ache.

Photos, as you know, have a habit of falling out of drawers, boxes and albums to remind us of the time they were taken. Orla's short time on this earth is marked now by just two photos, cradled in her mother's arms. She had just one summer then when we can recall so many. She felt the sun warm her pale skin for just a few months and she slept in her cot for just one Christmas.

We would all be out of our minds long ago if we were to dwell for too long on what might have been in our lives. But it does no harm at all to realise that every life has its summer light and winter shadows. I suppose it is how we cope with the bad times that is some sort of measure of our growing up; getting on with life while we have it.

The Way We Were is about that period in all our lives when parental guidance is most needed, not always heeded and then the day comes when we are alone to work things out for ourselves, on the trapeze of life without a safety net.

I suppose in their way, this book and the previous one, *All Our Yesterdays*, are retrospective compensation for all those unshed, lost tears.

Orla – in her mother's arms

A DELICATE BOY

My mother always followed the sun. You see I was a delicate boy and at my birth in the nursing home, the doctor, long gone to his reward, told mother that if I would see the teenage years I'd be lucky and I certainly would be gone by thirty. I do not know if they taught psychology to medical students in his time but his bedside manner left a lot to be desired.

A mother's heart is a fearsome thing and that bad news had just one effect, she was determined that I would survive, so she followed the sun. Each morning she would put me in the big pram with huge wheels, wrap me in a cocoon of blankets, pull up the big hood and clip the pram cover on either side so that all that could be seen would be the knitted cap on my head.

People would be still cycling to work to Fords and Dunlops or getting the bus into town, but mum would head towards Ballinure which was pure countryside even though it was only a few miles from the city centre. That was to the east and the road then was a twisting affair with great green fields, on either side of a few disused quarries, as this was limestone country. Over the railway bridge we'd go, beyond Ballinsheen and on to Ballinure itself with its big spreading trees and cottages snug behind big hedges, down between the tall estate walls to the Douglas River. She told me later that she would sit on a small stone fence and face the pram towards the sun, so that I could catch as much of the unpolluted, summer air as possible.

Home then at noon to prepare dad's dinner, as he would have just an hour to get back to work in Dwyers of Washington Street. Wash-up done and my brothers and sister gone back to school, the pram and I would be off out west along the Skehard Road, known then as the quietest road in Ireland, between more green fields, up the hill by Ravenscourt and down the other side to sleepy Douglas village.

All that fresh air must have had the desired effect as I'm still here to tell you about it, although admittedly second-hand, as you can imagine I did not remember those perambulations but would hear my mother talk about them many years later.

Having graduated from High Infants in the Ursuline Convent where I had kept falling in and out of love with the girls in the class and being totally smitten by a nun who always made me feel I was the only boy in the world, I moved to Presentation Primary on the Western Road. Now the rule of the school was that we had at all times to wear the purple blazer and on ceremonial occasions, the Pres cap with its hard peek down over the forehead. My mother always saw we had the best, even if she had to go without, so off with herself and myself to the shop in town, where my father, who was in the rag trade, knew we would be well looked after by the owner himself. My mother was rightly proud in getting me to the stage of actually going to a city school and the conversation would go something like this: 'He's lucky to be here at all, you know', she'd tell the man as he measured me up. 'The doctor told me that he would never make it; he had rickets you know and his head is still very small for his age'. To the credit of the man with the measuring tape he could see I was embarrassed, but did not want to be discourteous to my mother by ignoring what she was telling him. 'He's a grand lad now, he'll be playing for Pres before you know it.'

My mother would not be deflected; my story of survival was going to be told. 'I do not know if you will get a cap to fit him as he never fully developed as a child.' I'd be mortified but the man in the suit would continue and to my great relief a cap was found which was a reasonable fit, much to my mother's surprise.

The same story would be told to the principal in Pres and my mother's protective instincts would prompt her to suggest that I should stay in class during playtime. I often wondered what she would have thought when we would scrum down on the concrete yard and some would shout 'all a bah for a sweet'. Us lads would have slipped out to Peg's shop around the corner where the owner was like a second mother to us. On the little counter there would be a wooden tray of Thompson's fresh cakes and she would show enormous patience as we took her time picking out the biggest slice of donkey's gudge or cream doughnut. Outside the shop there would be another scramble as some would smash a blackjack bar into a thousand pieces and once more the shout would go up: 'All a bah!' If me ma could have seen her delicate boy then.

One boy and his dog

Love is blind

Iknew from a very early age that love was blind. One of my fondest child-hood memories was all about being ill. You see my mother's love was all embracing, a see-no-wrong-love. As I've been telling you, she was con-vinced that unless I was wrapped in cotton wool and shielded from anything that would threaten my health, then that would be that, her boy would not live to be a man. So, at the first sneeze, from the first cough, I was sent to the leaba and told to remain there until I was well again.

'You are not to stir outside the door,' she'd tell me before she'd leave to go shopping to town on the bus. 'I'll bring you home something nice from town, so stay there, keep the bedclothes over your shoulders, cover your chest and don't come downstairs if there is a ring at the door.

'The hall floor is very cold and you will get your death of pneumonia if you get out of bed. I'll collect your comics and if I'm not home before your brother comes in from school, make sure he makes you a hot drink. The Tanora is in the kitchen and he is not to take any of it for himself as I've told him that it's for you because you are sick.'

I'd hear the door slam downstairs and my mother's high heels clicking along on the footpath outside as she walked up Church Road to catch the double-decker to town. In a flash I would be out of bed and into my parents' room to gather up the latest *Woman* and *Woman's Own* and any other read-ing matter I could get hold of. My favourites then would be my mother's romantic novels. If she only knew she would have killed me as whenever we showed any interest in them, she would say: 'You are not to go near my books, they are much too adult for you, so don't let me catch you near them.'

This admonition ensured that at every opportunity I'd dip in when no one was around. Looking back now they were harmless but to an impres-sionable young lad those books from the little private library in town were exotic, a touch of the sinful. To be honest the dust covers of ladies with heaving bosoms full of harem promise were about the most exciting element as the stories were tame by today's standards. I would have to be very careful to make sure that mother's mark where she had finished reading the night before was not disturbed. I often wondered if she noticed that the pages would always fall open at the juicier passages of prose when the heroine would fall to the charm of the Bedouin tribal prince and they would embrace – 'wrapped only by the light of a silvery moon and a thousand stars'. My one fear was that the tell-tale Tanora fingerprint would give me away.

So there I would lie in a wonderland of eiderdown and soft pillows, a fire in the grate. Outside the frost covering the farm field would glisten in the weak January sun, the convent bell would peal and all was well in my Blackrock world. I would snuggle down and watch the fire's shadows dancing on the ceiling and think of my school pals in Pres getting their books out from their desks as classes changed.

Mother would come home from town. She'd feel my forehead. I could tell from the way she would look at me if I could get another day in bed. If she was worried she would send for the doctor. That was tricky as his diagnosis would be more professional and thermometers did not lie. If he declared I was improving then I knew I would at least get the week at home. I'd make a remarkable recovery for the weekend. My aunt next door would always say that being regular was the answer to all ills. Myself and the brother would always volunteer especially if we wanted to be off on the Saturday as Pres always had school up to lunch-time in those days. So we would manfully down the two tablespoonfuls of syrup of figs. Another aunt swore by senna pods. We'd suffer the discomfort the next day but feel it was worth it.

Getting back to my frequent bouts of illness, I would have to say that my father was less gullible and not as convinced about my state of health. When he would come in from work late that night I'd hear him talking to mother in the hall and then the great man would come up the stairs. I'd switch off the light and pretend that I was asleep. He'd go downstairs but if it was pay day, he'd always leave something at the end of the bed. It could be a toy farm-set or an annual.

Dads only pretended to be tougher than mums.

Mum, brother Terry and sister Mary

CHRISTMAS WITHOUT SANTA

I knew my brother had put his foot in it the minute he opened his mouth. 'I don't believe in Santa Claus, anyway', he told the table, well, not exactly the table, but my father who was, as usual, sitting at the top with my mother at the other end. She always kept us in check, so that dad would not lose his cool and ask one of us to leave the table.

My brother and myself had been rowing earlier about something and this was his way of getting his own back on me by telling dad that he no longer believed in the great one, the man who came out of the sky, down our well swept chimney and made our Christmas mornings.

Dad said nothing but you always knew when he was taking something in. A tinge of red would come to the cheeks, the brow would furrow a bit and he'd sigh. Then he'd look down at my mother as if to say: there will be more about this at another time. Dads even then were like computers, they had, and still have, a capacity to store material to be called up at another time. Dads were always ahead of their time.

'He's only jokin,' dad,' I said without any great conviction. My brother was in like a flash. 'I'm not jokin', I don't believe in Santa, so there,' as he smiled across the table at me with the look of a boxer ahead on points with the bell seconds away. I did not have the killer punch which would save the situation. The bell rang when dad left the table with the *Cork Examiner* under his arm. He asked mum to follow him to the sitting-room. I knew that was serious and glared again at my brother who left the table and headed off out the front door. He was always helping on a farm across the road and one of the sons had called for him as there was straw to be gathered after the threshing down the road.

That was October and I thought no more about it. Over the next few months I looked forward to Christmas; to Santa's annual delivery of 'something nice and a surprise'. As the great day came nearer I felt that not everything was right. Dad and mum would usually be joking us about Christmas

Day and we would be hinting at what Santa might come up with for two boys. We grew excited at the prospect of perhaps a bike or one of those wooden, pedal-propelled, go-karts which a buddy of mine up the road got the previous Christmas. It was only brilliant and you could whiz along the footpaths. With so little traffic then, he'd fly up and down our road too.

Christmas morning came and I must have been awake at the dawn. Usually Santa would leave our gifts at the end of the bed but there was nothing in the room. I did not panic but ran downstairs to check the sitting-room. There was nothing there. I tore up the stairs to my parents' room and told them that we must have been robbed.

My mother put her arms around me and said that Santa must have skipped our house because we did not believe in him any more. I was devastated; my brother was no better and we both sat on the stairs and cried.

Mother had brought us new shoes, pants and shirts with nice ties but we were inconsolable.

Santa and his friends

That Christmas, the first time we realised that Santa would not be calling to our house again, was the saddest of times. It brought the first realisation that we were growing up.

High notes from the hill

BACK TO SCHOOL

As a child I was not the most attentive in church but there was one time each year that the priest in the pulpit would put the fear of God into me. It was not hell and damnation, it was worse, he would announce that schools would be reopening the next day. I never understood why the adults in the congregation would smile at each other and nod their heads as if in agreement with the terrible news that had been delivered, it must be admitted, with some relish.

We children would wonder why our prayers had not been answered and the government had not declared a state of emergency, closing all schools until further notice. We did not wish any harm to anyone but always felt that six weeks was way to short and when we passed into secondary we thought that even eleven weeks was not enough.

What really got to me was the fact that the parents were so comfortable with the idea as if, in some way, we had been a burden to our mothers while on holidays. Sure didn't we sleep all morning and go to bed at all hours! I can clearly recall doing the wash-up and cutting the grass at least once every summer.

I often wondered too if adults realised how much we worried about things. Did old people every understand how things could play on a young person's mind? What if we could not find our sacks which we had dumped under the stairs in June? What if one of our favourite teachers had taken early retirement that summer? What if one of them had left the school that June saying he could not take any more and was taking a nice safe job as a lion-tamer with the circus? Sure anyway, didn't they always say to us that teaching was their whole lives. They might have added that we'd be the death of them but we knew all the time that they were only joking.

I'd be rich now if I had got a bob for every time my elders had told me that schooldays were the happiest days of my life. If they only knew how much we fretted; if only they could see things from our level, just a few feet from the ground. When I think of the pressures we were under all the way up the line. If we had just finished fifth and survived the Christian doctrine oral exam without uttering some heresy, then we were heading for sixth class and our first public exam before we launched into the deeper waters of secondary school education.

It was easy for dads and mums, they had no idea what it was like to cram so much knowledge into such a small space in so short a time. Did they not know that we had more important things to be doing with our lives? We had to be champion hurlers, Gaelic footballers and soccer players and all at the same time. We had to score the winning try for Ireland at least once every day. Sure in every match we played, there was always only a minute to go and our team were a goal or a point down and had to win.

Our dads must have got together because they were all singing the same September song about getting on in life and making the most of ourselves.

The boys of Cathedral School, Cork

POINTY NIBS AND INKWELLS

I can still smell school. The bus would leave us in town and rain or shine we'd walk up by St Francis church at the back of the courthouse, along Sheare's Street by the dairy, past the great houses and under the elm trees along the Mardyke. There was a drain down one side and we'd interrupt our journey to school to check what had fallen in or been pushed into the stream the night before; an old pram, the frame of a bike or a punctured football.

We'd gather in the yard and try and stay out of the way of the big fellows from the secondary. We were hardy enough and the odd skirmish would not always be a foregone conclusion. We'd manage an odd flick of the ankles and the trip was always timed just as the bell was about to ring and we could not be caught as we would be in our 'líne' where we could rely on the protection of the class teacher. The victim of our fun would fume, dust the knees of his long-pants and swear he would get us at the next break. It was these little extra-curricular activities which took the boredom out of school.

We'd climb the old, dark stairs of the primary school and head for our desks without a murmur as in those days a clip around the ear was expected and corporal punishment had yet to become an issue. We expected the odd clatter and some of us would expect to have to 'tabhair dom do laimhe' at least once or twice a day, depending on the humour of the teacher and our preparedness for class. No eckers done would certainly mean a flake of the thin stick across the hand or the leather would be produced and that was just as painful and effective.

When I think of it now I feel we put up with a lot and there was no way we would go running to our parents as that would be an admission that we were up to something and they'd back the school. I never ever felt damaged by such treatment as later on in life I would find that there were other forms of punishments other than a belt across the palms of the hands. Sarcasm somehow stung much more.

Even as youngsters we were no lily-white innocents and I'm convinced many a teacher was driven to distraction because of our mischievous ways. One sign of weakness spotted in the 'muinteóir' was quickly exploited to class advantage.

There was also the less identifiable form of punishment inflicted by pupils on other classmates. In those days the swot or even those making just an effort to keep up with lessons could be the target of what was in essence, bullying.

Strange though, this far removed, I have nothing but happy memories of school and stranger still are the things I can recall and those which have slipped from the memory.

I can still see the thin wooden-handled pens with their silver, pointy nibs and the little grooves in the desk where they would rest when not in use. On the desk too there was a round hole where the little white ink-wells would sit. We'd be given brown covered headline copies and it was no fun trying to write as, more often then not, the ink would run down the nib if overloaded and there would be a fine blob on the page. If we did not keep within the lines on the page, or if we formed a letter incorrectly, we'd get a right rap on the knuckles – so we got it right, most of the time.

But life does not stand still and we would graduate to the new building which housed the secondary and we would have to be wary of another generation of primary school-goers who would now see us as the enemy.

My fondest memory of school in those later years was heading for the bun-room at the break. Up a short flight of steps and resting on a tray on top of the little counter would be fresh cakes, especially ring doughnuts. The man in charge would pour the cups of tea from a great tin pot. We were getting used to adulthood and a visit to the bun-room was a more pleasant part of the ritual.

With the benefit of hindsight, it must be said we were blessed with our teachers. They made a huge contribution to the people we were to become. Religious and lay staff had dedication, the stamp of a true vocation which communicated itself to us. It stood to us throughout our lives. Not that all our hours in the classroom were always happy but we managed to muddle through – the brilliant, the not so bright but the willing. Exam time would come around and the boots and togs would be put away. The school would go quiet for a few weeks and there would be much head-scratching and soul-searching after each paper. The teacher would be outside the hall as each exam ended. He'd be a calming presence when we'd realise that we hadn't quite understood the question which had been asked.

We did not realise we were growing up and the carefree days were slipping away. Soon we'd be expected to be men of the world. Looking back, at this safe distance, they probably were the happiest days of our lives, though we'd be slow to admit it even now.

On a rare summer's evening, a few years ago, I was alone and back in the old school-yard where we sported and played. I thought I heard sounds of the past – a pair of leather shoes cracking against the footpath outside as the bell rang from within. Late, again, for first class of the day and 'the bus didn't come, sir', my only excuse. Through the open door-way and relief! The teacher is sick and first class is free – duck the copy-book winging through the air and watch out for flying ink-wells!

The principal appears at the door and the rest is silence.

Nightmare on the last bus home

It was a good time to be alive if you were a young lad. The war was over, the ration card had become a curiosity, the last coupons had secured the last half pound of butter; the gas masks had gone to the garden shed to disappear altogether with the next spring-clean.

Dad's man for the big garden at the back said that they were only in the way and we would never need them again. I was playing football with my brother when I heard that with surprising relief. Anything that threatened our little lives would keep me awake at night, looking up at the shadows thrown by the trees in the orchard. I'd curl up and wonder was Hitler really dead. If he wasn't, would he be hiding in Ireland? If he was, would he know that I was afraid of him as I lay in my bed in Blackrock? I'd roll over, curl up again and try to sleep. The one car to come down Church Road that night would have me wide awake. I'd wonder if that was Hitler, where did he get the car and who was with him?

Adults did not have a clue about the things which worried us youngsters to death. The lads in school were worse than the old ones as, if they thought that you were concerned about these things, they'd embellish their stories and tell you that Hitler had been seen in Ireland, much as we were told years later that Elvis was spotted after his death. The stories had no real effect in the daytime but when I was asleep I'd dream about being on top of the last double-decker bus home and hearing the conductor coming up the stairs, saying: 'any fares please, fares please?' I'd get out my tuppence and look up to see Hitler standing before me. I'd make to escape but my legs would go weak and I'd make no progress down the stairs. All the time he would be holding me back and I'd be screaming for my mother, swearing that I would never be bold again. I'd wake up in terror and that would be the end of sleep as I'd be afraid to close my eyes in case I would see him again.

I was a baby when we lived in a house nearer town but years after the awful event my mother told me how a fire in one room had destroyed her wedding presents. With that youthful contradictory disinterest in anyone's troubles but one's own, I did not give a thought for my poor mother but from that day I had an abiding fear of a fire in the house. When bonfire night would come around I'd only venture to the upstairs window and see the black smoke of rubber tyres rising to the sky. We were not long living in Church Road when the phone rang one night. My father was told that Grants on the Grand Parade was gone up in flames. I could hear him talking quietly on the phone as he sat on the step of the stairs near the landing. It was a blow to my father because there was some connection between Dwyers where my father worked and Grants. My father saw the fire as real tragedy as one of Cork's finest stores was to disappear.

I was a teenager when I saw the red glow in the western sky out our back window. It was the old Opera House on fire and the entire night sky seemed to glow. The building, which was so much part of so many people's happy moments, was reduced to an ugly charred shell.

It was like a death in the family for Corkonians and for all those visiting artistes who had trod its boards. Once again it was a blow to my father as he had gone to so many shows with my mother and also with his brother Paddy, both of whom loved the theatre and music most of all. Dad had given us, as a family, our first taste of that wonderful escapist world in that much loved building where cares of the day were forgotten when the curtain opened and a make-believe world took over.

My dad was a pragmatist by design but he had the wisdom to know that life needed its colour and romance and for an impressionable youngster it was good to forget for a while the imagined ghosts of war. When the Opera House burned down a piece of old Cork died in people's hearts.

The much-loved old Opera House gutted by fire

SINS OF THE PAST

We would be sent down to confession on Saturday morning even if we did not have a sin to tell. This was pre Second Vatican Council days and confession was a weekly affair; good for the eternal soul we'd be told at home and in school.

It's a wonder I did not end up with an attack of religious scruples as when I was caught for something to tell the priest I'd make up a sin like stealing six old pence from my brother. Then I was no sooner out of the box when I'd start worrying about the white lie I'd told. One time the priest told me I'd have to make restitution and I hadn't a clue what he meant. None of my pals had an idea either, so my brother remained unrestituted so to speak. But I did replace the six-penny bit with two English three-pences. An older brother told me that was 'restitution' and for years after I wondered why such a big word was used to describe just six old pence.

On certain occasions in school we would be marched down to confession in a city church. This was tricky as we had no idea what the priest would be like and what was his shock threshold. We'd sit in the seat and when the first lad would come out, he'd whisper to us whether the priest was nice or not. When I'd think of those poor men stuck in a confined space listening to a recital of our little misdemeanours for over two hours, I'd have the greatest sympathy for them. They were sorely tested as we considered confession as a reason to be out of school and we were going to make the most of it.

Once we switched city churches and when the priest slid back the hatch I found myself saying: 'Bless me father for I have sinned –' to a blank wall as I was faced the wrong way. My explanation to the priest was not really appreciated and he raised his voice to point this out. In a panic I came up with a real whopper just to get through the confession. I mumbled my act of contrition and stumbled out through the half-door into the light of the church, red faced and embarrassed. I had to go back to confession the following week and tell the priest about the lie. I heard a groan and even in the dark I could see the priest's head in his hands. I did not wait for absolution.

Lit candles and flowers on the altar to celebrate Quarant Ore

The green and gold in my life

It was my father first told me about the green and gold. It must have been sometime in the 1940s and I'd have been about five. He sat me down on a little wall, still there by the Atlantic Pond. He must have been afraid that I'd shout for the wrong team when he brought me in his arms through the turnstile at the Athletic Grounds on the showgrounds side. Dad preferred to stand on the open bank of shale and stone, where the Pairc Uí Chaoimh stand is now. Because I was so small he'd bring me into the side-line and sit me down on the wooden planks which passed for seats.

We were not long in the parish of Blackrock having moved down from Rosefield Terrace – that area next to Victoria Road was considered the parish too – just on the edge of Cork city. From the time he moved to Church Road, where my grandfather on my mother's side had built a house on the site of an old thatched cottage, my father became a Rockie to the core. He loved nothing more than to see them training in summer's evening in the top field bordering my granddad's land.

Dad had been associated with the Father Mathew Hall club attached to the Capuchins' Trinity church in the city. I was told much later that he fancied himself then as a trainer and would be seen with his team running along the Marina. I know his brother Paddy was an outstanding player and once, from a puck-out in the Athletic Grounds, put the ball straight over the bar at the other end. He was also said to have scored a goal from a puck-out in Dungarvan's Fraher Field. Paddy's son Michael, my cousin, would wear the blue of the Barrs and the red of Cork in hurling and football at minor level. Immediately after his Leaving Cert at Coláiste Chríost Rí, Michael went to America. He excelled in dramatic theatre studies before dying tragically in an apartment fire.

From my earliest days my father gave me that great love of the Blackrock jersey with its green and gold hoops. Myself and the brothers never missed a match. Blackrock seniors were in the doldrums then. They had not won a

Cork County Championship since the legendary Eudie Coughlan had led them to victory in 1931. It was to prove an end of an era for the most famous hurling club in Ireland.

My father would recall years later how Eudie led Cork to an historic victory over Kilkenny in a three match final. The first two had been drawn and Cork led by Eudie beat Kilkenny who had to line out without their injured star Lowry Meagher. Blackrock did not win another senior county until 1956 when the great Mick Cashman, father of modern stars Jim and Tom, led them to a first title in a quarter of a century.

In all those years from 1931, my father had a favourite hurler, a Kerryman by birth, John Quirke. He came as a ten month old baby to Blackrock. His father had brought his family from Milltown in Kerry to become a steward in the Ursuline Convent farm. John grew up in Blackrock surrounded by such great hurling families as the Coughlans, Ahernes, Deleas, Dorneys and O'Connells and hearing about the exploits on the field of play of the great Seán Óg Murphy and Jim Hurley. As a child then I would see my father's hero play against Glen Rovers in the 1948 final down the park and feel the heartbreak when the Rockies would lose again. John had to be satisfied with the county medal won seventeen years before.

I'd hear my father talking about the 1939 All Ireland final played in a thunder and lighting storm in which John played for Cork against Kilkenny. More than forty years later John told me about that match and how it nearly broke his heart. A mis-hit seventy yard free from Paddy Phelan, came to Jimmy Kelly who lashed it over the bar for the winner for the black and amber.

John Quirke had his own all-time hero, Christy Ring. 'He picked games out of the fire, he had the determination, the hurling. He would make the super-human effort and raise everyone else's game. In fact it was when I had left the scene that Ring really stamped his mark on the game. He got better and better, but was always great, even as a minor.' And John's 'greats' from other counties would include Paddy Cloghessy and Jackie Power, father of Kerry footballing star Ger Power.

The Munster senior hurlers of 1945, with Kerry-born John Quirke holding sliotar, extreme left kneeling, Christy Ring and, standing behind Christy, Mick Mackey

Which brings me to the other green and gold in my life. When I was very small I could not understand how another team called Kerry – and I would have to say, other names by my older pals – loomed large in my life. For some reason, which was never explained to me, dad always sat on the old stand side of the Athletic Grounds when Cork played Kerry in the Munster football championship. I'd notice that he did not have the same confidence in his stride as we walked down Barrington's Avenue and along by the pond before the Munster finals. We always seemed to play Kerry and I cannot re-call beating them too often. It is strange how the change of name could colour one's thinking. I'd be jumping off the seat when the green and gold of Black-rock hurlers would come running out but when the Kerry jersey appeared from the enclosure half-way up the pitch, my heart sank. My father, married to a Kerry woman, would be studying the teams in the programme and shak-ing his head. I took this to mean that we did not have a chance and to this day I will never forget the sight of those huge men from over the county bounds playing football like we played hurling, it all seemed so natural to them.

We always seemed to be living in hope of an upset and when it would come the faithful followers of Cork football would roar their heads off. I did not realise it then but Cork had won a marvellous All-Ireland in 1945 and my father would always tell me that Jack Lynch was not only one of the all-time 'greats' of hurling but a mighty man for St Nicks and Cork when it came to Gaelic football. 'He was a man who took on Kerry physically, he was skilful and fearless and had great leadership qualities on the field.'

It would be twenty-eight years later that another Corkman, Billy Morgan,

Homecoming – Jack Lynch [with trophy], Christy Ring and John Quirke with the victorious 1942 Cork Senior Hurlers – part two of the four in a row

would lead one of the greatest Cork footballing sides to victory in Munster and then take Galway in the All-Ireland final of 1973 under the guidance of the late and great Doney O'Donovan.

The Morgan name would haunt Kerry's dreams again, as a coach, as he took Cork to four All-Ireland finals in a row from 1987, winning two, in 1989 against Mayo and in 1990 against fierce rivals Meath in the second leg of the double.

In spite of all those defeats at their hands, my father never lost his love of the way Kerry played their football. Once they'd come out of Munster, he'd cheer them all the way to an All-Ireland. He'd died in 1973 and missed Cork's victory that September. I think too that if he had lived he would have rejoiced in the days when the kingdom of John O'Keeffe, Paudie O'Shea, Pat Spillane and John Egan ruled with devastating commitment and flair.

For my father the green and gold in his life had come full circle. He had handed on a respect for tradition which is savoured by his family to this day.

MATCH MORNINGS

No school time was ever as good as match mornings. For weeks before there would be the build-up to the great day. Even the staff would catch the spirit and there would be less emphasis on scholastic achievement and even an odd reference to the game. We'd latch on to that as anything that would distract the teachers from the impending exams would be a welcome bonus. Most of all we wanted to talk about our school's chances in the Munster Junior or Senior Schools Rugby Cup.

It was all a matter of life or death for those of us who would never make a first team place but saw ourselves as the greatest followers of the game. The fact that we could only see one team and had no time for any other was never admitted by us. A poor Inter or Leaving would be serious enough, we supposed, but to lose in the cups was the end of the world and there was no other way to put it.

On frosty mornings we'd be given an extended break. We'd be marshalled into the big ball alley in which I never witnessed a game of handball. On occasions, when the authorities were not looking, it would be used to play what could best be described as a game of risk. Well, that is something of an exaggeration but it was heady stuff all the same. Someone would get out an old golf ball and it would be thrown at the front wall. It would of course gather a momentum of its own and come flying back towards those gathered in its path. When I look back now I would have to admit it was foolhardy stuff but no one was ever injured. I suppose it was akin to the bravado of those who run with the bulls in Pamplona. There was more danger in being caught by the principal as word would then be sent home. There would be a chat between parents and then the head would talk to the culprits who would be in the bad books at home and away for weeks to come.

But back to the preparations for the big games and especially for those which would be played away from home against Rockwell in New Inn, Co. Tipperary, or with Crescent in Thomond Park, Limerick. As I say we'd all

Ray Hennessy of Pres leads the team out at Thomond Park, Limerick

Munster Schools Cup Final in Limerick, 1955 [Pres v Rockwell]

gather in the alley and be given song-sheets with the Pres clarion call 'Tango Tango'. There would be other less lusty, more melodic stuff sung with passion, if off-key, to such well known airs as the *Isle of Capri* or *The Shores of Tripoli*.

By the time match-day would have come around the tension would be mighty, there would be no study and no sleep for those travelling. Ten old shillings was a lot then but we all paid up and took our seats in the bus which parked on the Mardyke. Some of the parents were worse than ourselves and they would turn up on the morning to wave us off. We'd stick our flags out of bus windows and pass through Pana roaring our heads off. A few shoppers would smile and there would be an odd wave but generally our passage through the city would go almost unnoticed. It was only years later that we would realise that a school bus on the way to some match meant, and means, little to the uncommitted.

By the time we would reach the pitch, wherever it was, we would be hoarse but from the kick-off we'd never stop roaring. We'd have those wooden noise-makers which, when whirred around over the head, made the noise of a dozen corncrakes at dawn.

When the final whistle blew and if we had won, we'd charge onto the pitch like a purple horde with flags flying. If we lost, the depression would be down on us for days. The not insignificant thought would cross our minds that we would not get a half-day off school. We'd raise a few feeble cheers on the way home and only our mothers would love us by the time we'd reach Cork City.

Schools rugby days were all very triumphalist but we were young and could not envisage anyone being as good as us. Life would teach us otherwise and our partisanship would fade. Schools rugby was our whole lives and I often think of those who have worn the black and white with distinction and of those of my cheering friends who stood bravely by on the sidelines.

CHARIOT OF FIRE

May is a beautiful month. There is a freshness about everything and an exquisite sense of anticipation that the summer is going to be great. We conveniently forget that we thought the same the May before and were disappointed.

Wednesdays in May were always different from any other days because we had a half day. Once religious class was over, we'd tear down the Wessie and catch the bus to Blackrock from the Grand Parade.

In our house then, Wednesday was corned beef and cabbage day. Mother would stand over us – a neat, very pretty, woman and though small in stature, she had our respect, so if you like, you could say, we looked up to her. I can hear her voice now: 'Eat up now and grow strong like your father, the meat is fresh from O'Flynns in Patrick Street and the cabbage will keep you regular, I got it in the Market this morning.'

In the background *Hospitals' Requests* would be on the radio. Favourites would be *The Nun's Chorus* from *Casanova*. I remember getting a clip around the ear from my dad when I asked what *Casanova* was doing with a choir of nuns. It was years later that I realised my innocent question could have been misconstrued. If I had a pound note every time *Gold Thoughts on Golden Wings* was played, I'd be a rich man. In May the all-time favourite on the programme would be Canon Sidney McEwan singing *Queen of the May*. Dad would ask us to stop making noise while we ate our meal so that he could savour every note.

One Wednesday in May would have a different ritual. That was the day Pres College Sports would take place in the cricket grounds on the Mardyke. It always seemed to be fine on that day each year and rather then go home we would go straight from school.

I was no athlete but I enjoyed the excitement of the day and when the time would come for the sack race the tension would be mighty. Ever tried running in a sack? Well the knack was to hop along and just so there was some equality of standards with a minimum of agility, I could always bring down the likely winner with a lurch here and a lurch there. This was tricky stuff as the pre-race favourite would be supported by his parents so the trick

Chariots of fire – happy days along the Mardyke

was to make sure that this nobbling of the potential hero was done in the lane furthest away from the line of proud parents.

My mum would be there from the beginning but dad would come up from his work in Dwyers much later in the afternoon. It was just as well as I'm sure that he would have loved to see me win a few medals. We spend a lot of our lives failing to come up to expectations.

I was fairly handy at the egg and spoon race but was disqualified because sticking a piece of chewing gum to the inside of the spoon did wonders for the balance of the artificial egg. It did not impress the teachers. I wondered then if the philosophy of invention would ever take on with the authorities? I'd have a few uneasy moments on my dad's arrival when he would be seen talking to the principal. However, it has to be said, the man in the soutane was a good sort and never told on his students if it could be avoided.

There was the three-legged race when the school ties would come off and my pal and myself would become like Siamese twins strapped together. Co-ordination would not be my thing and we'd last a few yards before we'd tumble on the grass in fits of laughter.

My greatest moment came one year in the relay race when I was picked to run with a few flyers. By the time I got the baton on the final leg, the race was already over as they had gained such a lead on the others. But life would be nothing without the sporting chance and by the time we'd reach the finishing line the other teams of runners were up with me. I think the teacher that day had sympathy for me and knew I would be murdered for losing such a lead in so short a time. The verdict was that I had won by a chest. As I had a body like twine, I had reason to bless his generosity or short-sightedness or both on that golden day in May now so far away.

I was not exactly a chariot of fire but I was all heart. I walked proudly down the Mardyke that night between my proud parents with a little silver cup in my hands.

RED FLANNEL AND BOILED WATER

I had an auntie Nan who swore by red flannel and boiled water in the mornings. Whenever her sister Bridie, my mother, had a problem with one of us, auntie Nan would come up to the house from her shop next door and give her prognosis. She had remarkably clear, delicate, pink skin and she would always put that down to drinking a glass of boiled water first thing in the morning.

She never married. 'I could have had my pick of men in my time but I never did', she'd confide in me and would leave it at that, leaving a little bit of mystery in the air which I liked, as if I was her only confidant. She'd then turn to flick some imaginary dust from the sweet-jars on the shelf behind her and leave the silence add to that sense that she would not reveal all her life's secrets to a young impressionable boy. I was one of the family, her nephew, but there were things that even blood relatives should not be told. She'd turn, looking out the window and continue as if thinking aloud and not aware of my presence. 'No, I never married, but yes, there were men in my life.' Nan was an incurable romantic. I always thought she would not have been cut out for the day to day average relationship of a marriage but I saw her always as the heroine in the historical novel I would write some day when I was older.

When Nan would go on about the importance of wearing red flannel to ward off all manner of colds, my mother, who always had a thousand things to do, would listen quietly but her patience must have been tested. It would take more than unasked for advice and red flannel to ease the normal pressures on a mother of a young family of six.

There were times then when I'd notice a tension between the two sisters as if my mother slightly resented Nan's intrusion on what was mum's territory. My mother was a gentle woman but could, when the need was there, put someone in their place. They were next-door neighbours but their lives were world's apart.

Nan loved to tell me about the good old days and she would let me know that she did not always have to rely on the income from a small shop. God knows she was tied to it from morning to night and her only break came when one of us would let her take her tea at the back while we stood at the counter. I was a disaster at the job as I'd get into a total panic if a customer came and asked for anything other than the usual sweets or cigarettes. My younger brother was brilliant at it and he would usually be called up for tea duty.

As I was saying, Nan would, with the slightest encouragement, recall the good old days. Nan's brother, my uncle Jim, was apparently a brilliant man who had plans to set up a light engineering plant in the garden area behind the house. Tragedy struck the family when he died as a young man just when the foundations had been laid. With his death were buried the hopes of a bright future for the family.

Prior to his illness, life had been good to Nan and the rest with yachts being sailed from Blackrock down the harbour to friends in Passage. She'd remember wonderful Sunday afternoons when they'd laze on the boat anchored near Glenbrook. Then Jim died and Nan's dreams for the future were shattered.

Strange how all our lives hang by the thread of fortune and how little things like wearing red flannel and drinking boiled water in the mornings become important when the big picture fades.

GALA OCCASIONS

Bravado is your only man when you are under peer pressure. To survive in the classrooms of the 1950s you brazened it out or joined the ranks of the undistinguished, the also rans.

The *Penny Catechism* said that no lie was ever lawful but we would stretch the truth when it came to impressing those who were not easily impressed. Never was this truer than when the opposite sex were the subject for discussion. We had reached that awkward stage when it was necessary to exaggerate our exploits, rather than admit to our pals that we were in total awe of these creatures. We were in dread of our lives that it would ever be found out that merely holding hands and a chaste kiss were the sum total of our early teen experiences. We were at the nudge, nudge, wink, wink stage when we could not admit to our most sensitive feelings towards the girls of our dreams. We were sometimes guilty of telling howlers in order to maintain our place in the gang.

There were few enough chances to meet the girls at a social level in those days but there were the schools' swimming galas on Friday nights. For the entire week before, the chat between classes, during classes and when 'An Mhaistir' was not looking our way, was all about the gala coming up and the prospects for us embryo Casanovas to strut our stuff with the girls of St Als, St Angelas, Ursulines, St Brigids and St Vincents.

After school on Fridays we'd rush home and get ready for the nights of romance ahead. I'd dump the school blazer, don the jumper and flared pants, complete with colour clashing casual shirt. The hair would be doused in Brilliantine and parted in the middle. My mother would smile to herself and my father would say nothing and resume reading the paper. They must have wondered about their son who had suddenly taken a huge interest in swimming and was in fact getting a little bit out of his depth.

Of course the swimmers were brilliant and each race would be cheered to the last touch of the pool wall but the fun and fireworks were not con-

They're off – making a splash at a gala in the 1950s

In the swim – happy faces in the pool

fined to the pool-side as the noise coming from the balcony on both sides would continue long after the race was over or the last goal had been scored in the game of water-polo.

Now it must be remembered that we were growing up in a structured, monitored, age when meetings between teenage boys and girls were not all that frequent. Other than the gatherings in the Savoy cinema on Wednesday afternoons, when whole rows of us would enjoy the freedom afforded when the lights went down, we had little opportunity to meet away from the gaze of concerned parents. The galas for some of us were then a kind of free-for-all, a sociable scrum when nothing ever really happened but we thought we were particularly daring if we put our arms around the girl of our wildest dreams. It was essentially innocent but we thought then that we were the answer to every maiden's prayer, when in reality only our mothers could love us.

The following Monday, if we did not have school on the Saturday morning, we would embellish our exploits and claim that we walked some-one home and we courted on the way. The truth was more likely that we got as far as their bus-stops in town and just a peck on the cheek in gratitude for our gallantry.

MARCHING FOR GOD

A year in anyone's life is marked out by events which establish seasons, signal change and are associated with special times.

I always knew it was summer long ago when the priest would announce from the altar that the following Sunday the men and boys of the parish would be expected to gather outside the church and march into town in the Corpus Christi procession. It was the one Sunday in the year when there would be no talk of matches in the afternoon as the local GAA scene in cities, towns and villages would shut down in deference to the occasion – though some areas would gather and have their parades at noon.

There was, and still is, a very strong link between the Catholic Church and the GAA and that goes back to the times when Ireland was not master of its own destiny. Both organisations were seen as reflecting the right of a people to control their own lives. The establishment of a sovereign state would copper-fasten this bond and I can recall when an entire section in the side-line would be reserved for the men in black.

My father was a big man in mind and body and he would say that one afternoon in the year was little enough to give to a God who I believe was the motivational force throughout his life. Dad loved God and country with a practical fervour but not in an ostentatious way, so this was his one outward show of an inner belief.

I cannot recall at what stage I began to accompany him on these processions from Blackrock to Cork city's Grand Parade, a distance of over two miles, but I do know that I was not exactly bursting with enthusiasm. Previous to that my mother and the rest of us would have gone in early by bus to take up a position on the footpath in the city centre.

When mum broke the news to me that I was to walk with the men for the first time I could hear the snap of the apron strings and got an uneasy feeling that I was growing up and was not at all sure I liked the idea.

I was never an altar boy and never actually served Mass until I was in my twenties and a seminarian. Corpus Christi Sunday afternoon was the one day that I really wished I had been an altar boy as they got to wear the white surplices and carry the banners at the front.

We'd move off and after a while I got to like the idea of walking up the main road watched by the women and girls – the Church was then and, let's be honest, is still an organisation led by men – standing by the roadside. It is only in relatively recent times that they have been invited to march as well and it was not before time.

Rosaries would be said in a kind of a drone and hymns sung in that kind of apologetic way in the fashion of Irish men who have never accepted, as have the Welsh, that a voice in full, public, flow is the finest possible expression of the heart beating within.

My legs would be nearly gone by the time we'd reach the bridges of the city but my spirits would soar as we walked up the Mall on hearing the first faint strains of a brass band in the distance. It would be the Barrack Street Brass and Reed Band making its way over Parliament Bridge. It was a glorious sound as they swung into the Mall to our left and *Faith of our Fathers* would bounce off the buildings, the windows of which would be crowded with people who knew someone who knew somebody else who had an office or a shop on the route. Yes, there was an element of triumphalism but we did not see it that way. This was just one of the few days in the year when the streets were given over to the people, and for a young teenager it felt good to be with dad and older brothers and be part of an adult world.

The Blessed Sacrament would be carried through from Patrick Street by Bishop Coghlan, and in later years, by the legendary Bishop Lucey. Corporation Councillors and Aldermen and other dignitaries of the day in their flowing robes would gather round the raised altar at Daunt's Square. The smartly outfitted honour guard, complete with raised swords, would add to the pomp and circumstance of the occasion. Sermon and Benediction over, we'd walk back along the Mall and dad would buy us brilliant big ice-creams in the Cold Storage. They were so thick between biscuit wafers that our hands could hardly hold them and they had a unique taste which I have never ever found anywhere else. The made us forget tired legs and we'd catch a bus in Parnell Place back home to Blackrock.

Mum's Sunday teas were always special and she'd have made massive apple tarts but on procession Sundays we would not spend too long at the table as we would get out the bikes and cycle up the Dyke for the Procession Sunday tournament match. Instead of medals there would be suit-lengths for each player on the winning team and all the love of God and man would evaporate in the evening sunshine once the sliotar was thrown in amongst the two complete sets of forwards and midfielders. These would be battle-royal matches and the *Cork Examiner* the next morning would be full of pictures of the game and the procession.

The altar would be dismantled the next day and we'd keep our beliefs to ourselves until the following June.

The Host is carried from Patrick Street to the Grand Parade

I had no idea then just how great a responsibility it was for Dan and Ann to take me on holidays. Ann worried constantly and one evening she was given good reason to be so apprehensive. Around Ardmore Head, if you have the right local knowledge, there is a path down to an outcrop of rock called the cup and saucer because of their peculiar shape. Once down there it is great spot from which to cast a line for pollock in by the rocks or in August for mackerel. I have always had an abiding fear of heights and while I had no trouble getting down there, I totally lost my nerve on the way back up and simply clung face down on the path with the cliff's edge and a forty foot drop just inches away.

Someone must have told my aunt and uncle of my predicament as they rushed out from the village and out along the headland to where I was stuck like a barnacle to a rock. I heard my aunt screaming in terror above me but I was unable to look up and could not look down. It was a nightmare for them and because of their age they were unable to come down and rescue me. Eventually a passer-by heard the commotion and got me to edge my way up the grassy path to safety. There was silence on the way home and I was sent to bed without any supper.

As I passed through the kitchen I heard the radio announce that war had broken out in Korea. The door closed behind me but I stood in the hallway listening: 'That's the end of all of us, Ann, it will lead to another world war, I'm certain of that, God help America and her sons and daughters.'

'Amen to that,' Ann said and I could hear the wooden legs of the chairs scrape on the tiled floor as they knelt down.

'We'll say a decade of the rosary Dan, for peace in the world.'

I climbed the stairs and lay on my bed, starving, without my supper. I heard them going to bed in the room across the landing and Ann saying to Dan: 'I think he has learned his lesson, we won't ring his mother and father'. I thought to myself that adults were strange creatures. There was the world on the brink of war and all they were worrying about was my trip down a little old cliff. I fell asleep and dreamt of tanks trundling down the main street of Ardmore. The next day the tide in the main strand came and went without a hint of an invading force. I called for my pals and we walked along the coast, looking out for any strange objects on the horizon. A few days passed and we decided that Ireland was no longer in danger due to our vigilance, so we went fishing for cobblers in the Cove. Life had to go on.

Rock climbers on a summer's day

Sand-fleas and swallows

Nature knew summer had come before we did. A flock of starlings rose from the meadow, weaving against the cloud-grey sky, turning this way and that like a giant window blind, opening and closing, then letting the light in again. Down by the stony strand, sand-fleas hopped and bopped as the tide receded and they did whatever sand-fleas do when it was their turn to do their thing. On nearby rocks, gulls sat, beaks in chests, waiting for their curtain call. Aloof, doing a Garbo, was a heron, one leg in the freshwater stream where it gurgled through the white stones and etched its movement on the sand.

Across the bay an outboard motor punctured the peace as it putt-putted towards deep waters, voices from the boat carrying to the beach, a buoyancy of spirit reflecting the first nice day in weeks. Behind a tractor trundled across the field, sending up a diesel-blue plume which drifted then dispersed in the warming air.

Children twirled and swirled on the beach and with their bare hands dug tunnels and castles with moats and shaky bridges. Some chased each other and tumbled in free-fall, rejoicing in a freedom which would be theirs for so few years. Life, after all, was for children, and adults were there to provide. Those wonderful weeks would colour the rest of our lives. As youngsters we considered that everyone else was there to ensure that we enjoyed ourselves. It was not selfishness, just our way of seeing things.

After all, working all year at rearing a family or going to work could not have been as arduous as learning giant writing and sitting next to the girl with pigtails who wouldn't share her sandwich for a captive ear-wig. We thought that girls would never learn that life was all about catching things and keeping them in match boxes and swopping them for all sorts of things. Girls cried too easily when pinched and boys were always braver. That we would change our minds many years later would have been inconceivable.

As we grew older our adventures on holiday would become more daring. One day me and the pals decided that we would trace the source of that very river which ran into the sea. We did fine for the first mile or so when the tillage land opened up the bank on either side but soon the growth on either side grew more dense. Someone said that his father knew a man who once travelled up a river and was never seen again. He thought it might have been Africa but when someone said that he heard it happened in Ireland we decided to go back. My friend's little sister thought we should go on. It was the first time that my theory about boys being superior to girls was tested. Someone said that the next time we would go exploring girls should not be allowed. It was a case of if you couldn't win an argument, then you changed the rules, but time was running out for boys who would soon be men as swallows wheeled overhead and clung to the telephone wires before flying south in search of the sun.

Happy families – on the beach in Ardmore

HURLERS ON THE DITCH

My father would not allow discussion on politics. Well, that's not strictly correct, as I'm sure we did talk at the table about such things but myself and the brother were probably too young to get involved. Anyway, we would have been thinking about more pressing matters as to how Church Road would win the next World Cup against Ballinsheen in the big corner field on the road to Bessboro.

Later, in our teens, we'd be pre-occupied as to who was the lovely girl with ribbons in her hair passing down the road to Mass every Sunday. Remember there were few enough houses between Blackrock and Douglas, so a pretty girl was a matter of importance and we'd leave affairs of state to the elders.

I grew to like the run-up to election time and the more it was a village pump affair the better I'd like it. I remember one of my uncles talking about the days when there would be gatherings at crossroads, on street corners, and the agenda for discussion would be wide-ranging, from Ireland's neutrality to the arrival of a new priest in the parish.

Coming up to an election the gossip around the country would find a focus and the candidates would be assessed by the hurlers on the ditch. The seed and breed of the electioneering hopefuls would be gone through and there would be tree climbing as each branch of the family would come under fierce scrutiny. If there was a skeleton in the closet, the boys at the corner would have it or there would be someone who could fill in the gaps.

I would imagine that down the years pre-election conversations in villages and towns, by high walls and iron gates, would probably have run along these lines: 'Your man's uncle was a Free Stater although another brother was known to side with the Republicans. Then on his mother's side there was an uncle who joined the British navy. There was never much talk about him. He was killed in action in the First World War. They never found his body. Your man, the candidate, they say is the image of his mother and has a look too of the uncle who died at sea.'

Another in the group would be expert on the man's playing days as, if you could swing a camán or fetch the leather from the sky, then you were half way there, away for slates with the jury on the corner.

'He had an uncle who would have played for the county but he went away to study for the priesthood and Maynooth would not let him off from his studies.'

Another in the group could remember him and saw his chance to help complete the jigsaw. 'He was a good one. I saw him one day score a point from sixty yards and he down on one knee. You wouldn't see it today, I tell ya.'

The others would nod in agreement and matters would almost be resting so, when the Jonah in the party would inevitably come up with a conversation stopper, as if to introduce a note of reality, a sort of levelling of the playing pitch for the other candidates. 'His grand-uncle was fierce fond of the jar and there was a bit of a mystery about a grand-aunt too. She went away to be a nun and ended up in a song and dance show in the West End.'

The speaker knew that he had embellished the story considerably but it had the effect of getting his pals' attention and he was not going to waste it. He had a few bob on one of the others in the race and he needed to sway the electorate. 'My man would be a much better prospect, he has worn the jersey with distinction, all belong to him were out in the Troubles and he is great in a crowd.' The rest were a bit non-plussed about the reference to him being 'great in a crowd' but were obviously impressed with the other attributes.

Down the road, last Sunday Mass was over and the sitting TD, who was not liked at all by the corner boys, came into view with his handlers. 'Gomorrah men,' he said jovially and being never known to miss an opportunity of a vote, asked, as he passed by: 'Can I rely on ye on the great day, men?'

One of them spoke and the others nodded in agreement at everything said: 'Not a bother, if you are relying on us, you are home and dried. Sure haven't we always backed you and your uncle before ya. God Bless the love-ly man and wasn't it he who put the goal past what's his name when the parish won the county? Will we ever forget it and you with the generous father who filled our glasses for a week after?'

The TD moved on and smiled to himself. He was not codded by the lads and knew he would be lucky if he would get one vote out of the seven, but one vote was one vote and he forgave the lads their little deceit. He climb-

Electioneering when the horse still ruled

ed up on the back of the lorry and launched into an attack on the opposition. He loved this time when the minister would be sitting behind him and his people standing beneath him. He had an audience. This made up for all the times listening to people's woes, when he had to be all things to all men or at least appear to be so. This was his Tammany Hall. He would never now be a minister but these were his people and the ministerial presence cloaked him too in that attractive apparel of the inaccessible. Distance lent allure.

The lads in the corner had moved in the direction of the pub as the ministerial V8 sped by with the local TD in the back with the minister.

'Look at them, off to lunch in the convent, there is no separating church and state.'

Inside the pub the lads were told that drinks were on the TD.

'A lovely man, God bless all belong to him.'

Happy days in Taylor's Hill

Another sister of my mother's was auntie Kathleen. She lived in Galway when I was growing up in the 1950s. My sweetest memories of this warm and bright as a button woman, and of her husband Paddy Quigley, a handsome man with deep roots in Tipperary, were associated with the times I spent on holidays with them in Devon Park on Taylor's Hill at the edge of Salthill.

My mother would put me on the bus in Cork and I'd be met by my cousins Brian, Oliver and Jim. I was closest in age to Jim and I soon learned that he was already a hero amongst his peers. He was considered one of the most promising hurlers every to play with the Jesuit College, known locally as The Jes. Jim and Brian also rowed for this famous school. Like Christy Ring, Jim possessed a powerful pair of hands and wrists which could whip a hurl, as they are fond of saying in Galway, quicker than most. He would go on to be the youngest player to wear the Galway maroon in an All-Ireland senior semi-final in Croke Park against a victorious Waterford team though Jim excelled at corner forward. He later wore the blue of the Barrs and the red of Cork. Being Jim's first cousin from Blackrock had its advantages as Galwegians presumed I was as good an exponent of the fine art of hurling coming as I did from such a famous area. I was a very average player, a theorist rather than a practitioner but it was nice to bask in the reflected glory of my first cousin.

We were known to all as 'the cousins' and our days were filled with swims at the end of the promenade or when it rained, meeting the girls and going to the Astoria Cinema. My uncle was a member of the golf club, so we'd head off and many a ball I drove over the natural stone wall onto the road or over the rocks when to hit the fairways would have been much easier.

They were wonderfully happy days – Galway had yet to explode in size and everyone knew everyone else. The only time that things became really hectic were the days of the races out at Ballybritt when every hotel and guest-house was full and the pubs did a roaring trade. Auntie would put a curfew on us that week and we'd have to tell her where we were going after tea and we had to be home long before dusk.

She lived for her husband and family and was deeply religious but she had one other abiding passion, a political one I might add. She revered the Fianna Fáil party or rather its leader Éamonn de Valera. She would not countenance a word said against the man and her fidelity to his beliefs was expressed in many ways, not the least of which was that she would read no other newspapers but the *Irish* and *Sunday Press*. To suggest any other form of newspaper reading would be to invite trouble. Many a time her political beliefs would be called to question by relations and friends but auntie Kathleen was De Valera's staunchest defender and God help the man or woman who would in any way malign the man.

They were great and exciting times for us children in that cheerful, lively household which then looked out on green acres. We would never have thought that life would ever be otherwise.

Change did come and the cruellest of misfortune reminds me to this day that life's twists can cloud the finest of memories. My cousin Oliver, a quiet, gentle soul and a brilliant student, died after a short illness just weeks after he had begun his studies in University College, Galway. I often wondered if Paddy and Kathleen ever really recovered from that blow, though they would live full lives and influence us all for the good right into our own adulthoods. One would have thought that such a tragedy was enough for any lifetime but they would lose their devoted daughter Mary through sudden illness when they had come to rely most on her in their advancing years.

If we had any idea what was before any of us, we wouldn't leave our beds in the morning but seeing how others bear up to seemingly intolerable burdens, helps to sustain us all when the blows fall on our little existences.

The Quigley family in happier times

Off to Youghal

In my day the summer months were filled with tennis tournaments and cricket when we could find a spare piece of ground. We sharpened up our volleys and thundered down our serves in the junior tournaments around the county. To be honest we were not much good but we loved putting our names down for Sundays Well, Collins, Douglas, Church of Ireland, Rushbrooke and whoever would have us. They were our passports to weeks of lying around in the sun or, when the rains came, playing cards in the clubhouse and chatting up the girls.

My nearest claim to any sort of fame came when two of us reached the doubles' handicap final, much to our own and everyone else's surprise. There was only one problem, me, as I was over-age by a few months. Rather than risk the ignominy of being found out, we agreed that we should not turn up for the presentation at the tennis hop.

Rushbrooke was special but I cannot remember ever entering for a tournament which had that added pleasure of getting there each day on the Cobh train.

The best memory of all of that time was a trip to Youghal for the tournament in that historic East Cork town. We persuaded our parents to let us camp for the week and to our surprise they agreed. God love us, we had been molly-coddled growing up so this trip was the equivalent of a safari in Kenya. The rains came on the very first night and matters were not made any easier by the fact that we had pitched the tent on the side of the hill because we'd have a grand view of the bay someone had said. We bedded down for the night but someone remembered that one of the parents had given us a half dozen centre-loin chops to be cooked over a fire on the pan the next day. Thoughtful of them but not of us. We decided that the tent would be too warm for them so we hung the brown paper parcel from an overhanging furze bush. We forgot all about them as there were so many of us in the tent we had to take turns lying between two camp beds. No problem to a young

All eyes on the Number One Court at Sunday's Well

man but the problem was your feet would stick out through the tent opening, or for variety, you could help keep the tent upright by placing the feet at the top of the tent pole. I'd say we slept for about an hour in the whole night.

The next morning the sun was beaming down and we decided that some kind of breakfast cum lunch (we had not heard of brunch) would be in order and the chops would do very nicely indeed. There was a snag. The rain that night had washed away the wrapping and the rats had eaten the rest, all that was left was a bloodied piece of string. We were all sworn to secrecy and this is the first time that it has been revealed – given the time lapse, that's much as state secrets are released.

We may not have been great shakes at tennis but our cause was not helped when malnutrition set in by the third day. The tournament became secondary as one by one we were beaten by well-fed opponents who either journeyed to Youghal each day or were already at home. There was one high point of our day. Each afternoon those registered for the tournament were entitled to afternoon tea of milk and cakes. We were up to the clubhouse first and when possible we came back for second helpings if nobody spotted us.

Perks was in full swing then and we'd meet the girls as we sat outside Showboat when it was still a marvellous dance hall. I had heard my brothers and sister talking about Mick Delahunty and his band. I felt fierce grown up sitting there as couples passed by in their blazers and slacks, the girls with their floral print dresses swishing by on the footpath. It was heaven for a boy on the edge of life.

We were collected at the end of the week by our parents but not before a camp-bed had skidded through the back flap of the tent and down the hill with a courting couple on board. I do not know if the tent was much use after that but I remember it with fondness. Adulthood was beckoning and it did not seem too bad a prospect.

THE STARS LOOKED DOWN

She was my golden girl and I was a seminarian on holidays. I was totally taken by her beauty. I was no great shakes but they tell me clerical black attracts and who was I to argue? She was an au pair from Holland and we'd meet on the Main Street of Ardmore or on the beach and in that 1960s village we were something of a cause for minor scandal to some, though our conversations were as innocent as daylight. The topic was our shared passion for the music of Peggy Lee.

At the seminary we were advised not to make up our minds about our vocation during holiday time. It was suggested that we should head back to college before any decision was taken.

My mother, the wise one, sensed that there was something amiss. My father had returned to work in the city and I would drive my mother to the village and then earlier than usual in the evening, I would offer to drive her back to the holiday home. Once there I'd find an excuse to go back to the village in the hope of meeting the girl of my dreams. There were others of my age who were taken by her beauty and they wished I would disappear; read my breviary or do whatever seminarians were supposed to do on holidays. When they saw the two of us together so often, they too became suspicious.

While we were not exactly *Thornbirds* material, I did consider her a gorgeous young woman and I was beginning to feel the tension between wanting to be true to my calling and following the normal instincts of a growing young man away from the comforting restraints of seminary life. I was wondering if a life-time of celibacy was really for me and yet I had not the courage to make a decision either way.

We met one evening and I told her we would see each other on Tower Hill later. With mother safely at home and the rest of the lads dancing in Halla Deaglán, we headed for a field on the road to Ardho and sat on the grass beneath a harvest moon. Romance permeated the very air we breathed but I talked on and on about everything and anything. I was one nervous move from our first embrace and we had not even held hands before this, when the inevitable happened, I droned on about the next life as the stars looked down in disbelief.

Nothing happened and we said our sad goodbyes without as much as a kiss on the cheek. The next day she was gone home to Holland and I never saw her again. I went back to the seminary that September only to leave a year later.

On the way to Ardmore – obstacle course on Youghal bridge

HOME FROM THE HOLIDAYS

We'd notice it first when the dew on the grass in the mornings would turn to light frost; the nights would come in earlier and turn much colder. The frost would be followed by rain coming up from the south. There would be a wind and sea change, the ocean would swell, driven by an easterly wind and great mounds of seaweed would deposit on the sand, a calling card from a sullen, retreating tide.

There would be other things to remind us that the holidays were coming to an end. In mid-August, families, in Ardmore for a fortnight, would be seen packing up cars on the Saturday morning as they made way for the few who would have taken the second fortnight. But we'd cheer ourselves up with the realisation that there was another two weeks left before we went back to the city.

It was strange too but relationships between us boys and the girls would grow more intense; the initial shyness of the August weekend would have evaporated and we would be more confident. This intensity would not be world-shaking but we would have reached the stage that we'd risk holding hands in the main street. We'd sit on the storm wall with our arms around each other's shoulders. We would have got past the stage when we would tell the girls of our dreams that we would meet them inside of Halla Deaglán on ceilí nights. In the early years it would be in the old natural stone schoolhouse which is now a car-park space outside the church. Before that again we danced in the lovely wooden hall which was part of the Irish College, out the Youghal Road. We would have saved up enough of our pocket money to treat the girls at least for that one night in the month. It made us feel good.

As the final days slipped by, I would go into depression at the thought of Ardmore being over for another year. I do not know if it was the thought of getting back to the grind of school, the thought of losing summer friends for another year or plain being sorry for myself, as another summer romance was ending. I knew that I would not write though I promised to do so. I knew that when September came romance would be blown away as the reality of school and the coming year's exams would kill all thought of undying love whispered in the night, sitting on the pier beneath the cliff.

There was the empty bravado of us lads as we seemed to get up to more mischief in the final week. Orchards would be raided and we'd stay out all night watching for the dawn to arrive. It did, arrive that is, and we'd walk

Swimming lessons in the Cove, Ardmore, with the pier in the background

down the village with a swagger, thinking we were really wild and be disappointed when no one would take a tack of notice of us.

We'd walk across the beach on the final night and curse the invention of school. Fond embraces would be the order of things and we lads would struggle to hide our tears. We'd wish that we had never heard of girls and the way they had of getting inside our minds, making us forget all about such important things in life as week-long cricket matches on the beach; the Olympic Games held on the field above the strand and rowing boats across the bay or diving off Goat Island in Ardho. But there was no going back. In the girls of the time we had met our match.

The cricket bat and stumps; the hurleys and the soccer ball would have been packed by our mothers that final day. All that was left on the beach was the cricket crease and the stones which marked the goals for the World Cup final. This had ended in an acrimonious draw when the owner of the ball, myself, had been put off disputing a penalty. I did the only thing a professional footballer would do, I put the ball under my arm and went home. My father heard this and that was the last football to be paid for out of his pocket.

I hated the day we left the holiday home. All the thrill of going on holidays was wiped out by that one day when we realised that it was time to load up the truck with the bikes, the iron beds, the suitcases and my American uncle's portmanteau which weighed a ton.

We'd travel home in my uncle Paddy's car and we'd cry when Blackrock Castle would come into view as we'd pass Dunkettle. It would takes us days to get over the holidays but first day back at school, we'd have forgotten those promises of staying in contact with summer friends.

THE WAY WE WERE

Blackrock, Ballinlough, Ballinsheen, Beaumont, Ballintemple and Balli-nure were our rural retreats on the edge of a city not yet bloated, nor too full of its own importance. From market gardens to walled estates, wild meadows to Lough Mahon's shores, salmon boats bobbing at anchor by Marina's end as the first of the *Innisfallens* took lonely sons of daughters of the south to foggy old London town. Parents prayed by Penrose Quay that their darlings would write and be all right in a world of which they knew little.

The trams had made their way down to the pond, turned and trundled back to the city before the tracks were buried and double-deckers took us to the seaside and back to town, past great houses and huge gardens where now bedsits and semis fill spaces and overlook the Boggy Road for which there were once riparian rights. Here salmon swam under great limestone cliffs until they filled it all in and gentlefolk and gentry checked their race cards before Ford and Dunlop put their money on the assembly line. Cork grew rich and famous until the market changed and irons gates closed.

Fox and hare had swept over open fields, the rabbit, weasel, stoat and badger had the place to themselves until we, the only known tribe of short-pants Comanches, went on the war-path down by the woods and searched for pale-faces from across the river.

By stone walls we kissed our first kisses and wondered what was all the fuss when we could be spending our precious time fishing for tadpoles in the little pond in the wood but making sure we'd be home for a high tea of blacka jam and our mothers' rocky buns.

We'd know summer had arrived when they'd cut the first hay, toss it, turn it to let in lie in the sun before it would be raked and placed in cocks as bees would rise, disturbed and wishing we'd buzz off as we'd search for the corncrake or check ivy-covered walls for birds' eggs when there was no one looking.

Before corporate common sense prevailed and short-term gain would miss the big picture of DART lines and satellite towns, they closed down the little railway line which weaved its way through our Indian territory. Along by the river, past the Athletic Grounds, through proud Dundanion, on to the Black Bridge to swing into Rochestown, past Passage in the harbour and head upland for Carrigaline, then on to Crosshaven by the sea.

My grandfather told me that it was the sweetest thing to do – to catch

Tram at the terminus in Blackrock with refreshment rooms and horse-drawn bakery carriage in background

the train at Albert Road and head into the countryside, spending the day in Graball Bay, a pint in the village and home to granny's dinner of tripe and drisheen.

All my life, to this very day, I have wondered what might have been. If the line had been there we could have walked down the road and caught that train and we festooned with togs, towels, buckets and spades. We would have stood on the platform and waited to hear its warning whistle. Then we'd have stepped on board with a whole carriage to ourselves. We'd be proud as punch as, with our packed lunch, we'd sweep by Glenbrook and Monkstown, steal away by quiet Raffeen and in Crosser station we'd all step out for our day at the seaside. We never did that as they closed the line down before our time.

The wild flowers and hedgerows, the bóithríns and woodlands, the precious places of our carefree days have gone and there is little enough to remind us of the way we were.

LOVE AT FIRST SIGHT

I met my present wife at a schools rugby match in Limerick in the 1950s. That first encounter was to change the course of our lives.

We Pres lads would be heady with the freedom of a day on a train and the prospect of a Cup win. When we were victorious there was the triumphal march back to the train in Limerick and then the noisier march through the streets of Cork. We'd stop in the Mardyke at the back of Pres and would be addressed from the steps by the late and sorely missed coach Pat Barry.

On the day we had gone by train to Limerick, we headed for sausage and chips, no gourmet stuff for men at war. She was standing in the doorway of an ice-cream parlour. She was beautiful and with a Pres scarf wrapped round her shoulders, she obviously had taste. Here was my Juliet and I kinda hoped she'd fancy me as her Romeo. Her first words, however, were not: 'Romeo where art thou?' They were conversation-stopping nonetheless: 'Are my eyes turned?'

I was flummoxed. I had seen this lovely girl on the train and noticed that she slept for most of the journey while her pals from St Als chatted and generally ignored our efforts to attract their attention. I thought to myself that this girl standing before me now had a fierce look of Ingrid Bergman. With the male hunter instinct of a gangling seventeen year old I decided that she was the girl for me. Her opening reference to her eye turning was, admittedly, a bit disconcerting but I knew true love would find a way. I looked her straight in the good eye and asked her would she like another cone.

'It's the ice-cream is turning my eye.'

I decided not to pursue the subject.

The pals and myself met up with the girls at the match and in a fit of unusual daring I suggested that every time our team scored, I would kiss my girl with the cold eye. I was nobody's fool, as with the likes of Tom Kiernan and Jerry Walsh on the team, we were sure of kisses all round.

Coming home on the train we just held hands and cuddled up to each other but it was heaven on earth. They came through the train with the Munster Senior Cup and we wished the journey would go on forever.

Later that night in Cork, celebrations over, we said goodbye down the road from her parents' house. It was too early to give them the shock at what their eldest daughter had brought home. I was not exactly the catch of the day.

We kept meeting each other, going to the pictures and the rugby dances in Dolphin or in town after school. We were getting serious for two teenagers and I adored the ground she walked upon; she even got me to the Mother of Good Counsel Novena which would give you some idea just how seriously I fancied the girl with the ice-cream eyes.

That Christmas we arranged to meet in town and swop presents. I was building myself up to an inevitable meeting with her parents. Hard to believe now but to summon up the courage to go into a shop and buy a present for a girl was a major admission that there could be more to life than hanging out with the lads and playing football and hurling. Luckily I knew that my father was friendly with a nice man in Waters Chemists in Winthrop Street, so, red as a beetroot and weak as water, I walked up to the counter and asked if he had anything for my teenage … sister.

He was very understanding as he picked a nicely wrapped selection of Cussons' toilet soaps. I handed over the few bob I had and made a mental note to cancel the idea of taking her to tea to the Cosy Café on the Mall. I ran from the shop delighted with my strength of purpose.

Anne, the girl of my dreams was waiting under the clock at Mangans. I had the present behind my back and was about to surprise her when I heard the words: 'I'm breaking it off. I've met someone else. Anyway we were getting too serious.' My ears folded and the cap she hated fell down around my eyes. She just turned on her heels.

I swore that I would never love another woman again except, of course, my mother. I would join the foreign legion, a monastery, disappear on a ship to God know's where.

Anne never got the soaps, my sister did.

GOING TO COLLEGE

G oing to college was an understated disaster. Guidance was in its infancy. I wanted to be a chemist so I did First Science in University College, Cork. I should have gone to the College of Pharmacy in Dublin.

On such minor points great careers are thwarted. I had this vague notion of wanting to wear a white coat and look intelligent behind a counter. It was second only to my all-time fantasy of being a highly qualified, highly admired and highly aloof, hospital consultant who would sweep through wards each morning, nodding wisely and disappear at the other end. As to the prognosis of the unfortunate patients, I was not at all sure, but I would have settled for the admiration, the look of wisdom and delegate the minor matter of saving lives to the junior house doctors.

I've never been sure where all this make-believe had come from but I do remember seeing a *Carry On* film where a crusty James Robertson Justice, as the chief surgeon, asked one of his students: 'What's the bleeding time?' And the startled reply was – '2 o'clock'. I was hooked as I knew I had the bedside manner to make a great doctor.

Anyway, off with me to UCC with a barely-passed Leaving and a cobbled together Matriculation Certificate. I do not know if the National University of Ireland was ready for such an injection of genius but they need not have worried. My claims to fame at the end of the scholastic year were exemptions in oral Irish and scientific German. The oral Irish consisted of three of us sitting before the examiner and attempting to hold a conversation in the mother tongue. It should have been easy considering we had spent about thirty-six years between us learning Irish in the classroom. We were, I suppose, prime examples of the failure of the compulsory system. After a struggle we got through, having discussed in broken Irish the subject of hens laying eggs.

The exemption in German was necessary for the advancement to the second year. To this day my German consists of 'der Bunsen burner' but I do have the official note somewhere to prove that I had indeed passed through college that year.

But there was more to college life, as I'm sure there is to this day, than examinations. I managed to enjoy myself hugely at the hops in the Rest and was a bit player in the inter-society battles in the Quarry.

But the reality was that there would no cap and gown, no photos in the *Cork Examiner* on graduation day for parents who must have looked forward to that special day.

Half-way through second term I was noticed in the zoology class and was told by the lecturer that, as I was doing First Science, the reproductive organs of the frog would not count at exam time unless I was doing First Med. June came and considering that I was in the wrong faculty, preparing for the wrong career, I did not do at all that badly but did fail.

So, that first summer I said farewell to campus life and my parents, as always, hid their disappointment. They expressed the hope that I would find myself some day. I'm still looking.

All sorts of knowledge – lighting-up time at University College, Cork

Rag Week for University College, Cork students

What'll I do dad?

My father was a gentleman and to this day people speak in the warmest fashion about him. A big man over six foot tall, an imposing figure, his life was his job, and his job was, for decades, manager of Dwyers Wholesale Company in Cork.

My earliest recollection of the man and his work was hearing him humming to himself in the bathroom each morning around 7a.m. As he shaved, the humming would sometimes progress to a snatch of a song sung in a bass baritone voice. I knew he was a grand singer as when we had visitors I'd hear him do his party piece which was *Drinking*, the final phrases of which would descend into the lowest range known to human voice. My father would go almost purple holding the final note.

His singing, wonderful though it was, at that time of the morning would send me into the depths of depression as, once awake, I could not go back to sleep. I'd start thinking about the eckers which I had not completed the night before and that sense of panic about school would take over my thoughts.

I remember too that he would always sneeze twice and this would be followed by a short fit of coughing or clearing of the throat. It was years on before I realised that this reflected father's nervousness and apprehension about the day ahead. It hits us all but we don't care to admit it.

Anyway, the next sound to be heard would again be my father's voice as he would shout up the stairs for my brothers and myself to get up or we would be late for school. My father never drove in his life and he would be heading out for the early bus to town. When he did get a car he would rely on one of my older brothers to drive him, so all my life it seemed I would hear: 'Get up, I won't call ye again and if I have to go up to ye, then ye'll know what's what.' My brother loved his sleep and would hang on to the very last minute in bed. He'd try to fool Da by putting his hands in the shoes by his bed and lifting them up and down on the floor giving the impression there was someone moving around upstairs.

I'd leave dad in Washington Street and head up the road to school in Pres and I would not see him till around seven that evening. We'd all be sitting at the table for our tea, he'd look in the door of the dining-room and tell mother that he was going into the sitting-room to read the *Echo* while we finished our meal. When he did sit at the table with us, there would hardly be a word out of us, unless we were spoken to, and he would control the conversation. Though he was in his own time a fluent Irish speaker and a teacher of the language with Conradh na Gaeilge, I can never recall him speaking to us tré Gaeilge. I never understood this as I know he did attend the classes in the Irish College in Ardmore and worked to keep its doors open.

Dad, seated right, and his colleagues starting out in their careers

Even after a long day at work, dad's job was not finished as on Friday nights the Dwyer's travellers would ring him with their weekly reports from almost every county in Ireland. Mother would bring up a chair to the small landing half way up the stairs and he'd sit there for hours listening to their problems. He'd take notes to be acted on the following Monday, though he did work on Saturdays as well until one o'clock.

I have often wondered if the fathers of Ireland were not too taken up with their jobs and if too much was not left to the mothers in the rearing of the families. My father loved us all deeply and we wanted for nothing but even his precious summer holidays would be interrupted. He would put on a tie and shirt for the only time every August and walk across the beach to report to his boss who had a summer home in Ardmore. There they would, I presume, talk shop and father would only become his relaxed self again on his return home to the Curragh side of the strand where we children had the time of our lives every summer for over 25 years.

Dad wanted the best for all of us but had the wisdom to realise that what we did with our lives was really up to ourselves. In the 1950s there were not all that many jobs around, so knowing someone helped and would at least get you as far as a job interview. I had a Leaving Certificate Pass, earned by some effort of my own in the final year at school and great effort on the part of my teachers who were past masters at getting the not so brilliant to the finishing line, even if the rest were already in the winners' enclosure.

I did an interview for an insurance job, got it through my father's friendship with the manager of the office and then told my dad I did not want to do insurance. He said nothing but I would say my parents' prayers at bedtime that time included my future.

I spent the next four years in a seminary but decided against being a priest. Again dad put my happiness first but he must have wondered where I would find a niche in life. The *Cork Examiner* had a vacancy and a good friend of the family told my brother about it. I got it. My father's prayers were answered and Irish journalism's gain was the Church's loss or was it really the other way round?

WHEN JFK CAME TO TOWN

I joined the *Cork Examiner* in 1962 and could not be described as an instant success. In the *Examiner* there was little a cub reporter could do in the first year other than get to know the office routine and answer phones for those with more important things to do.

With the exception of a few visits to the courts with ace short-hand note-takers Sylvie O'Sullivan and Tom Barker, I was very much the office boy and not great at that either. We trainees also helped with the taking of copy that was recorded on red acetate that was placed on a cylinder and played back for typing up into hard copy. If the tapes were not marked clearly by yellow crayon then a story could go missing and it would be a visit to the board-room the next day. I was blessed in that my boss in the office was John O'Sullivan, a firm but fair-minded individual who showed a real humanity in his dealings with the new crop of reporters.

I remember one morning that John, as chief reporter, asked if there was anyone on the staff who lived in Blackrock and was in possession of a push-bike. I said I was and that was how I became the rowing correspondent for De Paper. I'm not sure what the rowing fraternity thought of the appoint-ment but as things turned out we got on famously over the years and it be-came a very happy time in my life. It was not without its mishaps as on the very first night I was cycling along the Marina, totally absorbed by what was happening on the river with crews in training, when I crashed into the back of a Volkswagen and landed on the roof of the Beetle much to the surprise of the courting couple inside. I never told anyone this before now but dis-tance and time does ease our embarrassment.

In 1963 President John F. Kennedy came to Ireland. For weeks before-hand there was feverish activity in the office as coverage of the great man's visit was arranged. I noticed that I did not figure in any of the diary mark-ings. John O'Sullivan in his kindness said that I could stand in Patrick Street and report what I saw as he passed along Pana. On reflection I realised that this was a way of getting me out from under the feet of those in the office.

I stood at the junction of Academy Street and Patrick Street full of my own importance with note-pad and biro in hand. I was ready for the most powerful man in the world and I was sure he would notice me at work as he passed by. I'd be there yet! Suddenly there was that whirlwind of expectation as the cavalcade came into view. There he was standing up in the open topped car with Lord Mayor Seán Casey seated below him. I will never forget the buzz as he swept by; in 1998 when the Tour de France came to town it did not match the wave of adulation which greeted Kennedy.

I was totally carried away. All professional restraint was gone and I ran behind the crowd to get another glimpse of the handsome bronzed figure doing Pana in the grand style. I cut through Marlborough Street to see him again as he passed along the Mall. I climbed up a railing outside some solicitor's office and blocked the view of those inside but I did not care. This time I was certain he waved to me. I jumped down from the window-sill and ran along the footpath at the back of the crowd in order to get across the bridge and I was going to try and get into City Hall itself. The young garda who blocked my way was having none of my bluster about me being an important reporter and that the next day's *Examiner* depended on me getting into City Hall with the other important people in the city that day.

It was about then that I remembered that I was to be back at the office typing up my story. For some reason not immediately apparent to me, nobody seemed to notice my prolonged absence and my major report never made the paper the next day. There were few if any by-lines then so I pretended to the girlfriend, her family and mine that my report was published all right, it just did not have my name on it.

John F. Kennedy was shot dead in Dallas that following November. I saw grown men cry in the *Examiner* Editorial that night.

Hail the President – John F. Kennedy in cavalcade through Cork in 1963

SUMMER SUNDAYS

The clash of the ash stirs me more than any sport. I have been known to get totally carried away when a good hurling match at whatever level is played with passion. The nearest I have ever reached the same intensity of interest would have been at schools rugby level which I have been telling you about.

I've told you too that because we grew up in the home of Cork hurling, Blackrock, and because my father ensured that he passed on the love of the game to us, it was understandable that my heart would pound when the club's green and gold or the county's blood red would sweep into view. It could be in Church Road, Pairc Uí Chaoimh, Walsh or Nolan Parks, Thurles, Ennis Road or Croke Park.

And so it is Sunday after Sunday, up and down the country, wherever the greatest amateur game in the world is played. I often think that the role which the GAA has played in our lives, especially for those belonging to rural communities, has not been fully appreciated.

For the real GAA fan, even for the sunshine followers and most important of all, the players, the championship season is paramount. Then all the preparation, all the slogging in ankle deep mud, the cuts, the bruises, the injuries, all pale to the importance of that first round outing when so much is at stake. The GAA season permeates everything from conversations after Saturday Vigil Mass or Sunday mornings when the next stop may the local pub, or if the match is away, it is a case of get on the road early, get there safely. The car parked, anoraks taken out of the boot, there may be time for a few scoops of malt or pints of the black stuff in Glasheens of Holy Cross, Bowes of Thurles, Langtons of Kilkenny, Ryans of Parkgate Street, Morgans of Cork. But more often than not, the Sunday game is an opportunity for a family to be together when God's half acre outside the town, any match town, becomes a picnic area.

The routine of rural households has been ordered by matches. Neigh-

Eudie Coughlan kissing the ring of Dr Hayden, Archbishop of Hobart, before the first replay of the 1931 All-Ireland final. Lowry Meagher, Kilkenny's captain, is on Eudie's right.

bours will milk cows for the man whose son is playing with the county. They will bale hay in Limerick and South Tipperary; pick carrots in Waterford; cut corn in Kilkenny or thin turnips in East Cork to ensure that man and boy are free for the fray the next day.

And then, in one game, it could be all over for another year. All the tactical talks, the 'listen hard lads' sessions in freezing dressing-rooms, the novenas with the girlfriends, the warnings about keeping the head from the throw-in, staying cool as the roar rocks the stadium in the first ten minutes, will count for nothing as nobody remembers a first round loser. But there is always the League and then there is next year and – 'God is good, the back door might be ajar if we can survive that first match and get a soft draw in the second'.

The GAA gave voice and identity to an oppressed people in the closing years of the last century and in the beginning of the twentieth. It was a force for good when few organisations represented the people's interest. Down the decades its role evolved to its present status as a unique national organisation which controls and promotes hurling and Gaelic football and to a lesser extent, but nevertheless equally importantly, camogie, handball and ladies football.

The days of the meadow field and stones for goal posts are all but gone; each area has its own playing complex; the corporate box is part of what we are but the essential truth remains the same, the love of hurling and football still beats strong in the Irish heart.

CHANCE OF A LIFETIME

My great-grandparents on my father's side came from a farming community near Ennis. My grandfather, a member of the RIC, was transferred to Co. Waterford, to Bunmahon, and then moved along the coast to equally beautiful Ardmore. His family lived over the barracks in the main street of the village with all its historic associations, overlooked by St Declan's round tower and cathedral.

Family history points up that chance is a fine thing. My father, Michael, worked in Cork, met Bridie Cotter, who was born in Killorglin Co. Kerry, and in the hurling-mad parish of Blackrock, they reared a family of dyed-in-the-jersey Corkonians. Dad's great wish was that he would see Waterford senior hurlers win an All-Ireland, and he did in 1959. Deep down he also wanted Clare, the home of his ancestors, to emerge as a force. I often think that if he had lived how he would have felt on that first Sunday in September 1995 when Clare ended their long sojourn in the GAA wilderness. I believe it would have been a proud day for him.

For those of us outside Clare, it is hard to imagine what it meant to its followers. In another code, when Munster beat the All-Blacks, there was a capacity attendance at Thomond Park, but as time went by all those who claimed to have been in Limerick would have not have fitted into the city, not to mind the ground. So it was for that fateful day in Croke Park. Many of those who did not make it to Dublin will some day tell their children's children that they were there when hurling history was made.

Clare's emergence as a real hurling force in the 1990s was the great sporting phenomena for this Corkonian in the final decade of the millennium. Those who count themselves as true sports' fans know that there is no pain as severe as the sense of continuing loss. Clare knew all that but never once lost their innate pride in their own. They saw great teams beaten in back-to-back championships; they saw their hopes die in the goal-mouth dust.

So 1995 was not just for the panel of players and mentors, but for all those who down the years had thrilled fans and neutrals everywhere. It was for the likes of Jimmy Smith, Matt Nugent, Seamus Durack, Seán Stack, Seán Hehir, Johnny Callinan and all the others who had never known the thrill of seeing a Clareman holding aloft the McCarthy Cup on All-Ireland day.

It was all the more remarkable that only a few years previously it was the county footballers who had shown the way along the rocky road to Dublin and proved that Clare was not just for the holidays, match-making and nimble-fingered fiddle players. After glorious 1995 then, Clare was not just for Merriman and Clancy, Doolin and Liscannor, Lahinch and Lisdoonvarna. For too long the county had to endure the haemorrhage of emigration, the flight from the land of its sons and daughters. Now it could hold its collective head high, and say: 'This is our year, our time has come'.

Brian Lohan and fan

At five o'clock on that special Sunday, when proud Offaly had to give second best, the Clare shout could be heard in New York. It proclaimed the dignity of a people who would never say die. The All-Ireland title, and the one that was to follow against Tipperary in 1997, thrilled Clare people in every corner of this island and the world over.

I thought of my father, son of a Clareman, born in Waterford, and ending his days in Cork, on that Sunday evening in 1995 when I walked Curragh Beach in Ardmore. I knew for sure that he would have been happy for the Banner.

Anthony Daly returns home in triumph via Shannon in 1995

SUNLIGHT OF OTHER DAYS

'It's not the same.' It was a little old man sitting on a bench. The annual regatta was in progress. 'When I was a boy, the world and his wife stopped for the regatta,' says he, half noticing, half ignoring me, as I lent the bike against the back of the seat and sat down beside him.

'God, I will never forget my dad walking me from the northside, down the hill from our house, through the little lanes. As we'd pass the neighbours, I'd tell them I was going to the regatta with my da. They'd shout back: "Good on ya boy" and my mother would be calling out to my da, from the wall above the path, to take good care of me and not be stopping in the pub on the way home.

'Across the city with its Saturday traffic, we'd spot the side-car at the quayside. Da would lift me up in his strong arms. I'd sit in his lap as the man with the cap would flick the reins and we'd be off.

'We'd pass by the old mills and the coal ships with the dockers' faces all black as the coal dust swirled up from the holds. My da would spot some of his friends and tell them he had taken the day off and that he might see them later for one. I did not know it then but "one" stood for a pint though I can never remember it being "one" but it was never less than two and usually more. My ma would be cross about that and be going on about him drinking his wages. But later I'd see them hugging and kissing in the pantry and I loved when they did that.

'We'd turn left off the quays and then left down Fords Road. I snuggled into my dad and hoped that those walking under the leafy branches on either side would realise that this was my dad and we were going to his regatta. We'd pass the factories and reach the Marina with the sweet stalls and racing boats to my right and up towards Shandon the enclosure.

'I always thought my dad was important but I was never so sure when a young man stopped him at the gate and asked if he had a pass. I did not know it then but my da had a drinking friend who was a member of Shandon and he spotted the two of us. He dismissed the young man and called to my da: "Come on John, the two of you are very welcome. How's the care and is this your young man you are always talking about? Come in the two of you." I was ten feet tall to think my da was so well known and so famous.'

The old man rambled on and I wondered if I should do what I was supposed to be doing, covering the regatta for the *Examiner*. If I went he would not have even noticed but I wanted to stay.

'Then there'd be a brass band playing between the races and if you had the right ticket you could get tea and sandwiches in the white tent set on the other side of the path. There'd be a line of bookies and the lads from Trinity and Queens in their blazers, white pants and shoes would be putting there last bob on the Leander Trophy race. Before the races started from the stake boats opposite Blackrock my da brought me over to see the trophies set on a table covered in a white cloth. There amongst the huge cups and shields, the Leander ship stood tall, waiting for its new holders who my da told me years later would not always take great care of it. I hear now they do not even give it to the crews but keep it safely from year to year. What are things coming to at all?'

I told him I would have to be off and check the results.

'Off with ya boy. I'll be going myself soon, I'll wait for the Leander. I remember going home with da was great because we'd stop a few times on the way and he'd be flying by the time we'd reach Shandon Street. There'd always be a sing song and my da would sing *Thora* and *Silver Threads among the Gold* and they'd be roaring for more. My da and myself would head off, careful to slip quietly past the neighbours' houses or they'd be talking to my ma the next day as she headed for early Mass in Pope's Quay. Safely home we'd have a feed of rashers and eggs or if ma had been down in the market that day, da would have a feed of drisheen and a bottle of stout. They'd send me to bed and I'd hear them laughing up in the kitchen.

'When my da died there was no one to take me to the regatta and now when I go myself I think of him more than at any other time of the year.'

He got up and shuffled off along the footpath to the city, not even notic-

ing the Leander race passing by on the river but recalling the sunlight of
other days.

Tivoli view – Cork Regatta, when crowds gathered on the Marina and across the river

THE PATH OF LOVE

It must have been a shock for Anne's parents when they saw me but, to their credit, they never let on.

I had driven down from Cork city to Guileen, a lovely little seaside village to the east of the Cork harbour. It was not so much my appearance, though I could hardly be described as dashing in rainwear two sizes too big for me. The ensemble was topped off with a black helmet which again could not be described as fitted.

It was the bike which must have made the lasting impression on them. It was, in fact, a scooter, painted blue and yellow and on one side there was an entire panel missing. It had started life quite a different colour but the previous owner may have been from Tipperary and had opted for the county colours. It looked fine on hurling jerseys but it was strange livery for a scooter.

I had been courting Anne for a few months after I had returned from the seminary and she had come back from Romford in Essex where she had been a student nurse. We had taken up where we had left off as childhood sweethearts. My mother always felt we had planned our return to Cork in the same week but it was a coincidence as we had not corresponded when I was away studying for the priesthood.

I had been kept up to date about Anne through mutual friends. I did see her one night at a New Year's Eve party when I pretended not to notice her when in reality my heart was pounding and I just wanted to tell her how beautiful she looked.

How many times in all our lives do we say nothing when a few brave words could change our destiny. Anyway, I did sing dumb and went back to the seminary. Now here I was making a decidedly uneven first impression with the two people I needed most of all to impress.

There should be a manual brought out for parents for those great moments of stress. Here they stood, meeting the man, the boy, who would, unless fate intervened, carry off their precious, eldest daughter. But parents can be brilliant and they never said a word other than that of welcome, though I did catch Anne's father taking another backward glance at the scooter by the wall and shaking his head as if in disbelief. He had made his living, earned his daily bread, with his hands and he must have wondered what kind of a husband would this young man make if this was his mode of transport. He must have wondered too what had happened the side panel and I would have told him, if he had asked, that I had no idea. I would have suggested rather weakly: 'It was like that, Mr O'Connell, when I got it.'

Gilbert was always a man who kept his thoughts to himself and would never have hurt the feelings of his beloved daughter and therefore the scooter was not really discussed that first summer weekend.

The great loves of my father-in-law's life were his wife Ita, his daughters Anne, Frances and Ena, his job, his dogs and fishing. As a young man he loved nothing more than to get out on a Sunday in the countryside for a bit of shooting or fishing on the Bandon River, or later in life, fishing off the Pollock Rock, south of Poer Head, near Guileen. I remember clearly how he would come into the house on winter Sundays and the first thing he would do would be to disarm the gun and put it away safely, out of harm's way.

Gilbert had another passion and that was music. He loved opera and opera singers. He had his favourites amongst them. Up there at the very top were diva Maria Callas and tenor Jussi Bjorling. I was always trying to impress him and he would enjoy playing various pieces of music and getting me to guess their titles. I'd bluff for a while and he enjoyed catching me out, but he could hardly have realised that he was in the process giving me a love of the very same music which continues to grow to this very day.

THE HONEYMOON

Looking back now, getting married in the early 1960s in Ireland was quite a traumatic affair. At the time it did not seem so, but marrying a childhood sweetheart, with both of us in our early twenties, was really a leap of faith in the future.

Hard to compare times then with things as they are now – they were different in so many ways. I think we were courting for about twelve months before Anne and myself became engaged. The ring, a good one I hasten to add, cost about £60 and was bought in Roche's jewellers in Patrick Street in Cork. The time of engagement is a high point for the girl with pals making wishes on the ring and going into female huddles into which a male dare not enter. I assured myself that I would remain the same. There is no lack of commitment but the males like to think that nothing has really changed.

We became engaged on an August Saturday so we began the day by going to Mass in St Mary's church on Pope's Quay. Anne said it was traditional to do so and who was I to argue? I actually liked the idea myself. Mass over, hand in hand we walked along by the river, crossed Patrick's Bridge and in with us to Tivoli Restaurant near Mangan's Clock.

God we were the innocent souls as we thought the world knew we were engaged and we wanted the whole world to know it.

Anne's parents were on holidays in Guileen and mine in Ardmore. We decided to ring them both with the good news. Now I have to explain at the outset that my mother loved Anne and I sometimes wondered if she thought I was not good enough for her. However, knowing how she had cherished me from the moment of birth, the thought should never have crossed my mind. Anyway my mother did harbour the idea that my leaving the seminary two years previously was in some way connected with 'my grá' for Anne. There was no telling mum otherwise. It might have been the Kerry blood coursing in her veins but mum said things as she saw it and she would never 'plamás'. We phoned Ardmore with the news of our engagement and the first question was: 'Why, do you have to?' Anne loved mum and at that moment her love was tested; she came through with flying colours.

We married some 14 months later and when I see marriage ceremonies now I wonder were we married at all. There is now so much emphasis on the couple as the celebrants of the sacrament. There is such a sense of commitment and involvement between priest, couple and even congregation. It is in a language that everyone understands. In our time you would have wanted to be a high scholar, though we were used to hearing the Latin Mass every Sunday. The priest had his back on the audience and we youngsters wondered when it would be over so we could head off with our pals down the Marina; down the village of Blackrock to the Pound or down the Bessboro Walks for chessies. But I digress, we did get married even if it was all in a sort of haze. The only moment of that special ceremony which now comes to me is the sense of panic when I put the ring on the wrong finger. The rest is something of a blur.

Reality prevailed once again when we headed for the reception at the Country Club overlooking the city we both loved and still love so well. It was one of those pet autumn days, truly the last roses of summer blooming against warm walls. All our friends and relations were there and I remember my favourite of all-time uncles, uncle Pa, sang his party piece *Trumpeter What are you Sounding Now?* My genteel auntie Nan tut tutted but Pa was in full flight and there was no stopping the Little Corporal who had seen duty in the Troubles and had earned our admiration and favouritism down all the years because of his gentle, kind ways.

The honeymoon was something else. Dad, God bless him, had given us his car for the duration so we headed out the twisty road to Mallow with tin cans trailing and toilet rolls swirling in the wind. We must have been a sight but we thought the world was ours and sure it was too. We were heading for Galway – none of your exotic islands in the sun in those days. Everything went well till we got to Ennis in the dark. I took a wrong turn and we were half way to the Cliffs of Moher before we realised it. I did the thing males do when they are wrong, blamed someone else, so Anne and myself had the

The girl I married

first silence of our marriage. We eventually got to Galway about 11pm and found our hotel, the Sacre Coeur, in Salthill.

The first night of any honeymoon has its nervous moments and I again did the manly thing once we had reached our room – I went downstairs to the bar for a pint of Dutch courage. I got talking to what I thought was another nervous young man. I confided in him and presumed he was in a similar position. The next morning at breakfast I saw him smiling knowingly across at me from another table. He was in his tour guide uniform and as he shepherded his elderly American charges to the coach outside he passed our table and inquired if everything was to our satisfaction. I studied the grapefruit segments and his comment elicited Anne's first question of the day for which I had no answer: 'Who was he?'

Galway in that October fortnight in 1964 was heaven on earth as we danced to the Miami and Clippers, saw the autumn sun sink, turning the Bay into shimmering flame and walked beaches with only herring gulls for company. Too soon it was over and we headed home with £5 in my pocket to go towards my first car, a showroom Morris Minor bought for £250 in the Central Garage then in Parnell Place. Later we'd buy our first house with the help of a Corporation loan for £2,300. Those were certainly the days.

Postscript: The reception for over 60 people at the Country Club cost £80.

No traffic jam here as cars wait in the wings

Time out in Galway of another era

THE MAN WHO MISLAID HIS WIFE

It seemed like a good idea at the time. In the big smoke for a weekend, a wedding of friends, then a day in the Dublin mountains and the piece de resistance, the All-Ireland hurling final on the third day.

As I say, it seemed like a good idea, but as the poet said about the best-laid plans, they gang aft agley.

We, that's the wife and myself, reached Henry Street in comparative safety and having got over the initial shock of seeing everybody walking in the middle of the street – this was the 1970s and Dublin had long since wised up and kicked all the cars back into O'Connell Street – we headed for a well known store where we knew some friends. She who must be obeyed went straight to the changing-room to put on her maxi for the wedding.

I paced the carpeted floor outside the ladies changing-room for what seemed like an eternity but was only about ten minutes, then another ten and another and no sign of Anne, that's the wife. I began to panic and decided to ask the supervisor, who was swinging a returned bra like some giant sling-shot, if she would be kind enough to go in and inquire as to the health and present state of my loved one. She did but did not. You see Anne had left by another door without my noticing.

The supervisor with the loose bra returned not at all sure about the nervous gentleman who was looking for his wife in a brown maxi on a hot stuffy, early-autumn day. The chase was on. I do not know if you have ever tried to find someone in a store of three floors, one-way escalators amongst a seething mass of plastic bags and parcels. For one panic-increasing hour we searched for each other. I admit all these years on that the wife was the more resourceful. She had the intelligence to make several announcements over the public address system asking an unheeding public to give her back her husband. But I ask you, do you heed every call coming from ceilings and pillars when out shopping? Well I did not and the hunt continued.

It was at this stage that I decided that my wife might have gone into the street in search of her hero. Palm-lined Henry Street had now become, in my fevered state of mind, a jungle on which a September sun beat down.

A maxi in a mini-minded world should not have been hard to find but it was another hour before we were united. At this stage two young gardaí had become suspicious about the man who had mislaid his wife. They found me in an oasis of potted plants sitting with the people for whom life always seems to pass by.

Our troubles were not quite over as we had to get to the church in a Dublin suburb in thirty minutes. I thought my wife was a bit unfair suggesting that after all that fuss I could have at least ordered a taxi to the wedding. I thought the double-decker bus was brilliant. Ever noticed that silent journeys tend to take that much longer!

MAN OF THE ROAD

The old man, stubble beard, cap, pipe and oily Aran sweater, under seam busted overcoat, pulled together by twine, looked down on the beach below from his grassy perch on the cliff's edge.

'God, doesn't the sunshine do to people what it does to insects? They come from everywhere and beetle about, going nowhere.'

'You from these parts yourself?' I asked.

'Well, you could say that, and then again, you could say that I'm not, if you follow me.'

I didn't but it was worth trying.

He went on. 'Everything has changed. I can recall hot summer days when the gentlemen would shy at taking off their coats and the women wouldn't open the top button of their blouses lest they be considered vulgar. Now sure, anything goes.'

'I suppose it's the way we are, progress you might say,' I suggested not very convincingly.

'Oh, don't get me wrong. I've an eye for beauty for myself but there was a lot to be said for the old bit of mystery, the buttons and bows, the chantilly lace did a lot for a maiden who nature had not endowed of its own accord.'

'You have an eye for beauty,' I said.

'You might say I had and then again you might say I hadn't, then again!'

'You've known a bit of romance in your time,' I suggested, not sure how he would take it. He was still a handsome man, strong face with high cheek bones and piercing blue eyes under bushy brows. His hair was grey, almost to his shoulders. He had the broadest shoulders I had ever seen, even allowing for the baggy clothes. His hands were like shovels and he had the long fingers of a classical piano player.

'Were you married yourself?' I ventured.

'Why is it in this world that everybody who has reached a certain age, is expected to be married. Some of the happiest people I have ever met were single, and by their own choice I might add. And that is not to say that a life on your own is a passport to happiness. There are times when I'm walking the roads that I see a little cottage at the foot of some mountain. I wonder what it would be like for the farmer to walk up that lane-way of an evening, having checked the sheep and fed the few cattle in the lower fields. I'd be thinking that it would be grand to walk through that half door and be met by a smiling woman, my children at the table and a blazing fire in the grate. That would be heaven.'

'Life on the road is lonely then.'

'You could say that but then again!' he thought for a moment. 'Then again I get to thinking that I could be all wrong. What if that home beneath the mountain is an unhappy one. I think that maybe the man of the house or for that matter, the woman, is looking down the road at me and thinking to themselves what they would give to be free like myself, not a care in the world, the open road before me. The longer I live the more I believe that happiness comes from within, being happy with your lot.'

'You're a bit of a philosopher,' I suggested gently.

'You could say that!'

'So, you never married?'

'I was once. God she was gorgeous and I loved her so much. She was a raving beauty and we had a great passion for each other. We met at a dance in the local hall and we only had eyes for each other from that first old waltz. She was like a feather in my arms and later when we held each other close and kissed outside her widowed mother's home, I told her that there would never be another in my life and there never has been to this very day. We married two months later.'

'What happened, did she die?'

'No, not at all, it just didn't work out. Her family never had any time for me and they turned her against me, though God knows, I did not help things. After two years I got the old hunger for the road. Anyway the little farm could not sustain me and herself, her brother and mother. One night

I just got up from the bed, kissed my sleeping beauty on the forehead and took off, as simple and cold as that. It would never have worked and we both knew that, we were in love with the thought of being in love rather than with each other. Life is much more about wet Monday mornings than Saturday nights with a few large bottles and a dance with the girl of your dreams.'

'Did you ever see her again?'

'No, the last I heard of her she was in America married to some professor in one of those big universities. I heard she came home for the funeral of her brother – her mother had died a year earlier – and the selling off of the home place. I heard that she called to the local pub with her three grown-up children. The eldest is supposed to be the image of me.'

'He could be yours!'

'You could say that, but then again!'

With that my man of the roads was heading across the fields to the main road west. I thought about the mother of three in campus America.

Chicken, chips and peas, please!

I should have known there would be trouble ahead. My eldest child was already showing leadership qualities at the age of five.

It was the 1960s in Cork and a sign of the times was the opening of the Talk of the Town grill in the Savoy Cinema. Upstairs there was a grand restaurant which looked out over the canopy and into Patrick Street. Here generations had met and shared happy moments in plush surroundings, enjoying the luxury of being waited upon by a staff who would know the regulars seated at tables with neat tablecloths. Going to the pictures was the social event of the week and having a meal was part of the night out.

But change was coming and The Talk of the Town was a signpost to that. It was down a few steps along the passageway to the stalls, a new place which reflected the move towards a less sedate and more in tune place to go for the younger set. There was the long Formica-top counter where you could sit on high stools or there were tables surrounded by modern tubular-style chairs. Eldest daughter climbed up onto on one of these chairs and agreed to sit quietly and not to talk to anyone while dad headed for the gents.

'I won't be a minute, love, when I come back we'll have lovely sausage and chips for daddy's little princess.'

Princess was not listening, she was busy looking around the glass and plastic palace and smiling at the waitress.

'Don't worry about your little girl, I'll look after her,' she assured me and I headed for the toilet.

I was just on my way back when I bumped into a former school pal of mine and we chatted for a while before I went back to the restaurant area.

There she sat with a big smile on her little face, a paper napkin tucked under her chin and the clear line of tomato sauce around her mouth. In front of her was a large plate of chicken, chips, peas and a big glass of orange. There was more bad news as there was another plateful at my place, a pot of tea and two snowball cakes on a plate in the middle of the table. Just as I sat down the smiling waitress brought a large bowl of ice-cream topped with fruit and melted chocolate. 'The nice lady said that I could have whatever I wanted and I told her that my daddy had a big job and he would pay for everything when he came back from the toilet, so I did.'

I was speechless and she took a deep breath and was off again.

'She said that I was right to have what ever I wanted and that I must have been a very good girl to have a father who would bring me for chicken, chips and peas. Wasn't I good daddy? I did not talk to anyone except the nice lady who brought me all this food, so she did – am't I a great girl, daddy and I only five? Mammy will be proud of me, won't she daddy, so she will, cos I was very good. Amn't I daddy's little girl?'

I had ceased to hear my little treasure as I was mentally totting up how much I would owe. I had a half-crown in my pocket and at a rough estimate the bill would come to about five bob.

'Eat up your chicken, chips and peas, daddy, cos mammy said that we should always eat everything on our plates if we wanted to grow up big and strong like you daddy.'

I rummaged through pockets in the hope that I would find another coin which would save me from the embarrassment of not having enough to pay for the heap of food on the table.

'Daddy, can I have more orange from the nice lady? Daddy, why are you not being a good boy and eating up your chicken, chips and peas?'

'Daddy is not feeling too well and has to go to the bathroom again, love, you just wait there and daddy will be back in a minute.'

I had seen a gangster film where the good guy had escaped his captors by climbing out through a toilet window. I decided against it as Princess was still in the Talk of the Town finishing off the chicken chips and peas before she got dug into the ice-cream. I decided to face the music and tell the waitress of my plight.

'Daddy, look at me amn't I a good girl, I've eaten all my chicken, chips and peas and now I'm eating my ice-cream, will you tell mammy what a good girl I am, won't you daddy, cos I'm your princess, amn't I daddy, amn't I?'

The chicken, chips and peas girl

Then the penny, or rather the half-crown, dropped on the floor. It had slipped through a hole in one of my coat pockets. I reached into the other pocket and there was the original two and six. I was saved. I paid the bill, all four shillings and with dear daughter in my arms, I ran down the steps into the fresh air outside. We got the bus at the Statue and daughter had the last word when we got home.

'Mammy, we had a lovely time but daddy left all his chicken and chips on the plate. Sure he won't grow up to be big and strong, sure he won't mammy, sure he won't?'

The Savoy Cinema, once home of the Cork International Film Festival

THE ODD SOCKS MYSTERY

I hate Mondays with a passion. First day of the week, at work, at school, down the mine, up in the clouds, wherever, Mondays are miserable and things happen on Mondays.

Take a pair of socks, or rather, find a pair of socks; more to the point, find a pair of socks that match. In our house there is a large plastic shopping bag which is a repository for socks made from all types of material coming in all sizes and colours, but they don't match.

In our house on Monday mornings five pairs of feet seek socks. It is then the sifting of evidence begins. It has never been explained to me how socks, down at heel, or just after their very first spin dry, can separate and never come together again.

In our house there are thick socks and thin socks, long and short, wool and polyester, but, having started their lives, stapled together and in the first flush of parenthood, they no sooner have had their first spin in the tub together, then they separate and are never seen together again, at least not in our household.

Winter mornings are worst of all. First the alarm fails to go off and the bathroom is booked out. Then the search for the socks begins. Could it just be built-in obsolescence? Why do a perfectly normal couple of reinforced woollies disappear and leave not a trace behind, not a stray thread.

Have machine manufacturers come up with a wash-programme which drip dries one sock and shreds the other? Or, is their merit in the theory that it goes back to Celtic times when, on certain days, our ancestors wore one sock as a mark of respect to denote their position in the clan.

Of course, it may only be a good yarn.

THE QUIET MAN

Isaw him first standing like a solitary crane bird on a glistening black rock as the surf swirled round him. He was motionless, the stiff rod an extension of his two arms pointed high over the turning tide waters. They told me in the pub up the hill that he was all his life in the merchant navy and he had a spare, ship-shape look about him. I never saw him without a pipe in his mouth. He never seemed to fill it but was always lighting it and little puffs of smoke filtered out from beneath the neat moustache, the hairs of which were brown at the edges from the hot stem.

I had tried for four cold, early summer evenings to catch my first bass from the same rocks on which he now stood. I had heard about casting out beyond the partially submerged rocks and letting the circular lead bring the line back towards the deep pool where the bass lay as the fresh stream water mixed with the angry, salted ocean.

I watched him for hours, never taking my eyes off the rod or the holder but I still missed it. I came round behind along the cliff path and there it lay in a shallow pool above the last high tide mark. It was a bass about 10lbs in weight. I had seen the old man arrive at his rocky perch and yet missed the moment when he had whipped the rod in the air and struck the bass, the hook catching in the roof of salmon-like mouth. It was all so clinical, so matter of fact and yet it would take a lifetime to capture the art.

I first met this spare-rib of a man, hop-stepping across the rocks a field away from his home, nestling on the sea side of the hill. I had been waiting in ambush for him ever since they had told me in the pub that he was the man for the soft crab-bait, which the bass loved. He stopped and spoke, never looking my way but out to sea at some imaginary ship on the horizon. He told me that I would get the bait if I met him the following day. At last, I thought, I'd learn his secret, I'll find out where he finds the crabs in black, gurgling holes under rock and swaying seaweed. Of course it was not to be. The jeweller shapes the diamond, the potter throws shapes in quiet studios.

True artistry is not an overnight thing and knowing the dark lair of the soft-back crab is learned over a lifetime and not for the sunshine, come-day, go-day fisherman of one summer. When I met him in the cove the crawling harvest lay in the bucket with the wire handle, kept fresh by weed and water.

That night I stood on the rock just near him. He with his bleached stick and line and I with the latest sectioned rod and reel with 20 lb gut strength. I'd be there yet before I'd get even a bite as he hauled in two silver beauties in the first two hours. He left me there, announcing as to himself that there would be no more fish caught that night. I stood there for two hours more, my head-torch flicking light on the waters below. I headed home frozen to the bone and boiled the crab bait and ate it.

He's gone now and his secrets have gone with him and it makes you wonder about life and all that cannot be learned from books alone.

No flies on the lads

(as others see us)

The Christmas lights have been taken down and the wise men out in the Lough have gone east – no flies on them as a north-westerly swirls around Pana.

Even Women's Little Christmas is over, the last gin and it, the final vodka and lemon have been downed.

The strings of tinsel, the funny hats, the bugles and the crackers lie with the fairy-lights box in the bin in the yard.

The crib has returned to the attic and the non-shed-tree is leafless in the yard. Its stand has already been lost as it went out with the first refuse removal after Christmas. It's being so organised keeps us going.

Dad says soon we will be cutting grass. He's right, we'll be cutting the grass as the 'old back injury' will keep him off the lawn. He can still hit a fair old golf ball and flick away an imaginary leaf from its line to the hole in the centre of the green. Different sets of muscles, he says, as he sits there and wonders if anyone was making a cup of tea and did anyone see the paper.

First son says to second son: 'Let him get it himself,' but mother has heard and first son hands father the paper before he is parted from the hair on his head as mother sweeps by.

They say that Christmas is a wicked time for family quarrels but January must surely be worse as all goodwill has been dissipated and it is time to resume normal transmission.

'There's a stretch in the evenings,' father says.

If there is, it is not so much that you would notice as occluded fronts play piggy-back out in the Atlantic and storm clouds gather over the city like giant spaceships.

'Before we know it will be spring, then Patrick's Day, then Easter and we won't feel the summer creeping up on us – then we'll be talking about Christmas,' father says.

'*Carpe diem,*' school-going son suggests.

Father looks puzzled, returns to reading his paper, wonders but says nothing – a case of never letting the enemy know what you are thinking.

Mother enters and says tea is ready. 'It's on the table and you are not to eat it in the sitting-room. I'll bring yours into you, love,' says mother to father.

'You're a little treasure,' says father.

'You're a fool for him,' says one son under breath and the other for once agrees but says nothing.

'We must take a break, love, we must take a break, it would be good for us to get away from it all for a few days at this time of the year,' says father.

Big day for the boys by the Lough – the game is on as Jack Lynch throws in the ball, with great theatre man Danny Hobbs on standby

'You're right love. I'd like that. I could do with a break. Where would we go?' says mother.

'I thought Killarney would be nice, I could bring my golf clubs,' says father.

'But I don't play golf,' says mother.

'You can always caddy for daddy, love!' says school-going son, again under his breath.

'What's that son?' asks daddy.

'Nothing daddy,' and buries himself in his comic.

The man from Valparaiso

That day they had carried out his coffin along the wind-swept road and laid him to rest in the sodden sad earth. The man who had travelled the world from Valparaiso to Sydney had come to rest a few miles from where his journey had begun eighty years before.

I heard of his death on the hour the bells tolled out the old and rang in the new, as lovers kissed, promised to love no other, as resolutions were born, to be forgotten by hang-over morn.

His passing should have meant nothing to me as paper bugles tootled in my ear and the drunken strains of *Auld Lang Syne* blared around the hall. But the news stopped me in my tracks as dancers weaved by and the band played – forever and forever.

The last time I had seen him he was shuffling the stone floor across a shaft of sunlight which had momentarily pierced the back-window and lit the room to the half-door. It was one of those strange July afternoons when brilliant sunshine conjured up rainbows with sudden showers as sullen clouds brooded over distant hills. A thunder cloud melted overhead as rain-drops slipped from the straw-ends of thatched eaves and a harvester droned in a nearby field as giant wheels bogged down in the soft earth.

I moved slowly by his gate in the hope that he would talk to me about his travels around the world but I had heard that he was shy of strangers and kept himself to himself.

He was his parents' pride and joy, had excelled at the local national school and helped his mother around the house. He would row the wooden boat out beyond the surf-covered rocks as his father undid the tangles in the hand-held trawl line. The one lobster pot would be baited and dropped outside the rock line before they'd head across the bay for the pollock and cod grounds beyond the point. There they would rest as his father lit his pipe and the youngster trailed his hand in the deep green water.

He'd ask his father a thousand questions without waiting for the answers as young boys do. Gulls would do a spot check and sweep away when they realised that the day's fishing had not begun.

His father would take the two oars in big palms and draw them back through the tide as the trailing line sank in the wake of the boat. The boy would stop talking, look at his father and pray to himself that he would catch the biggest fish his father had ever seen. Some days they would do well and fill the wooden box with its rope handles, other days they would catch little, but everyday they grew closer to each to other without a word uttered to draw attention to the fact.

The lad, then fifteen, told his mother first that he wanted to join the merchant navy and one night as they knelt on either side of the bed, mother told father of the child's wishes. The father simply nodded his agreement and they lay awake all night thinking how short a time they had with their fair-haired boy.

The son would come home once each year and tell them of his travels, the places to which he had been and the people he had met. He did not tell them that he had cried himself to sleep every night in his bunk on that very first year away from home. He did not tell her that the beautiful white shirts and vests she had bought in the town for her little lad had been strewn across the cabin floor on the first night at sea. Someone had joked on the ship that this was his initiation into the real world.

The boy from the thatched cottage became a man, fell in love in many a port but never married. He would come home twice with a heavy heart to bury first his mother and a year later his father who they say had died of a broken heart. The next day his son burned the little rowing boat in the back-yard and came home just once again to live out his retirement from the sea in the place where he had been happiest.

As an old man, he could be seen looking out from the headland to the place where once the pollock and cod teemed in green waters.

The band played *Waltzing Matilda* but I was thinking that Valparaiso was a long way from home for a lad who was only fifteen.

Tall ship in a safe harbour

WOMAN OF THE WEST

The woman from Connemara would always be leaning over the half-door with a fag between the fingers of the right hand, her face lit by a smile as she greeted the passers-by. Time had become her own and she had time for everyone.

Her friends would be invited inside for a cup of tea and a slice of cake. The smoke would swirl up to the low ceiling from the open fire which she would stoke up with a long blackened poker. She would sit on the low, three-legged stool flicking the ash from her Woodbine into the fire.

She was in her sixties and still very beautiful. The hair was natural grey, the only blemishes were the eye-brows and roots at the forehead which had been browned by the cigarettes. Her voice too had been affected by the chain-smoking and every now and then, the hand would go to the chest as she went into a coughing spasm. She had know better times but never said so, never complained, she had a full life and would not diminish another's by the even the hint of complaint.

That beauty of her's had broken but never won men's hearts. She had that indefinable Garbo mystery about her. She had lived and loved but was now alone, no one with which to share the memories of a life full of promise never quite realised but still not regretted.

Her day would begin with a prayer on her knees by the bed, a wash in cold water, dressing, still barefooted on the cold stone floor and then a luxury, a long leisurely combing of the hair before the cracked mirror.

Outside then in the ritual search for eggs in the little out-house by her thatched cottage which nestled between great boulders, sheltered from the Atlantic gales. She knew all the hiding places and would show visitors how to remove the still warm egg from its resting place without disturbing the laying area as it would be replenished again the next day by the few Rhode Island Reds, survivors too of bitter winters and uncertain laying seasons.

And there was another luxury. She loved to boil an egg for herself, cut the batch bread into little 'saigdhiuirí' as her mother had shown her all those years ago and dip them into the soft yoke. She'd wash it all down with a cup of tea which tasted as no other in the world. Then the fresh bastible cake would come out, it would be cut with the big kitchen knife and great slices would be covered in the farm-churned, salted butter.

She'd return to the fire, turning the bellows wheel and lighting up one fag after another. She'd remember how she first set out for America. She travelled through Galway, noticed how the land grew softer and greener as she passed through counties Limerick and Cork. She thought that Cobh, then Queenstown, was a city itself with its fine, terraced houses and cathedral looking out across the harbour.

She stayed alone in a rented room and cried herself to sleep.

She woke before dawn, looking out through the high windows of the guest house and seeing the tender tied up at the quayside below. Her parents had given her all they had so that she could escape the poverty of life on the land. Her head looked forward to America but her heart was at home.

Her mother, father, younger brothers and sisters could not afford to travel to Cobh to see her off. Her mother had held in her arms for hours the day before she left, cradling her eldest and telling her to be careful and to keep herself to herself until she got to know people and even then to be careful. Her mother's tears flowed as she felt the frustration of warning her daughter about a world of which she knew little or nothing.

The girl's father had stayed out in the little reclaimed half acre all that last day, tears in his eyes as he knelt on the dried seaweed which crackled with his weight. He kept himself occupied weeding around the spindly potato stalks which were hardly worth earthing up. His knees were protected by two sacks tied with binder twine but his back was breaking and his heart broken. He went inside, picked at a meal of salty bacon, late spring cabbage and the last of the old potatoes. He could barely look across at his daughter.

Before she said goodbye to the family, she walked with him down the bóithrín to the rocky cove for the last time. They said nothing but it was still

Thatched Cottage by Cloda Hassett

the closest they had ever been and would ever be together. She placed her two hands on the keel of his upturned currach. It no longer went to sea but they had shared some happy moments fishing off the headland when she was a child. She'd sing at the top of her voice some Irish song she had learned at school and he'd pretend to be cross with her and tell her she was frightening the fish. They were the good times too but they had been too few and too many things like, 'I love you dad', never got said.

They walked back and, outside the cottage, he put his hand on her shoulder, went as if to say something but could not. He simply patted her on the head for a second and said he was going to see if there was a rabbit in the snare.

Her father would be dead within months of her landing at Ellis Island. Neighbours told her that he was never the same when she had left for America. Her mother would pass away two years later.

The brothers and sisters would join her in Boston and she would be the only one to come home to live again in the family home.

She never said it but the story was that she had been unlucky in love and could not bear to be in the same city, the same country, in which her lover lived with another.

Outside the wind was blowing with the kind of fierceness only experienced in the west. She walked beyond the low, natural stone wall, down the lane and lit up again, looking out across the slate-grey waters. She stood there most evenings on her own, her hair blowing in the wind, sitting on the now rotting, upturned currach and she would think of what might have been.

Then one morning the neighbours found her lying face down in the kitchen. The still warm egg lay cracked on the floor.

COOKING UP A STORM

It was far from barbecues we were reared. If my father had lived to see one of his sons standing under a umbrella, setting burgers on fire, he would have said nothing, kept himself to himself, but wondered where did he go wrong.

There is something in all of us which draws us back to the time when primitive man – I take it there was a primitive woman too – headed off into the woods and returned with an unfortunate wild deer over his shoulders. He would then intone to his family gathered around the fire that it would be 'venison tonight'.

I take it that the high kings of Tara and Knowth thought nothing of throwing a few wild boar on flames and announcing to their Wilmas and offspring that there would be no need to go to the cooler in the bog as there would be spare ribs for everyone in the audience.

One of the great culinary feats I believe is to ensure that the sausages do not fall between the bars of the griddle, into the white embers below. When you have allowed only 16 sausages for family and friends, then extricating the burnt offering may be a necessity.

Part of the joy of cooking out of doors for some must be the inhaling of the billowing smoke but for me it is the sense of control. I've never been comfortable in a kitchen though my white stew has been acclaimed, well, I've loved it anyway. I have to admit though that my efforts at mixed grilling in the open air have not always met with instant approval.

There are precautions to be taken and the first is to make sure that your nearest and dearest, particularly the young, are kept well away when daddy is cooking up a storm.

There are moments of real drama which stand out in all our lives. I begin all my barbecuing with the sermon on the griddle about the necessity for caution by my children and their captive friends who sit listening at a safe distance.

One day I got particularly carried away by my own eloquence and in the best traditions of orators used my arms to make a point. I happened to be holding a bottle of uncapped liquid fuel in my hands and managed to spray the already hot coals. The flames shot into the air and I fell over a chair in my haste to avoid being incinerated with the sausages.

The children thought it was the highlight of their day and one of my own suggested that I should do it more often. Apart from some singed ivy on the back-yard wall, there was no damage done but she who must be obeyed pointed out that if I talked less and led by example more, our children and those of our friends might live a bit longer.

I've always had difficulty with the logic of women and I'm even more troubled by the fact that they are invariably right.

Great cooks are proud people and well they might be, but I've always felt that I too have been something of a spoiled chef. My greatest happiness is to see others delight in my expertise.

There is too a stubborn streak in my kind and this almost ensured my demise and arrival in the land where good chefs go when their last pancake has been tossed.

Good friends and relations, who were worth impressing, arrived one afternoon and I saw my chance to whip up a few delights out of doors as the sun shone in a cloudless sky. Irish summer Sundays are nothing if not unpredictable and as I prepared to lay the last of the sirloins over the white heat, a chill breeze swept by and then from nowhere, dark clouds loomed up from the west. Before you could turn a rasher, there was mighty clap of thunder. My youngest, who was learning the culinary art from the great one, told me the story of how someone in South America had been hit by lightning.

'It struck the fork in his hand, dad, and all that was left was one shoe.'

I wondered where the dear boy got his information but continued on with the umbrella over my head. All the others had by now retreated indoors and watched me cooking outside. I'd be there still, rooted as it were, if she who is obeyed with good reason, had not come out and marched me inside. When I suggested that the one thing, in my opinion, which women appeared to lack, was the sense of adventure, she looked at me with what could be described as steely resolve and told me that if I did not behave, I'd be sent to bed without any supper. You'd swear I was one of her children!

Eating out with summer friends

THE SINGER NOT THE SONG

I walked Raglan Road and Clyde on the night Yehudi Menhuin died. I thought about the joy the maestro brought to so many lives.

I passed fine houses, embassies and flats where still reside the rich and famous. I thought too about Monaghan's Patrick Kavanagh and the Dubliner Luke Kelly.

I remembered my friend Henry Curran who was Kavanagh and Kelly in one; a Waterford word-smith who riveted disparate hearts with his poems and songs. He was Henry the First for all; the first to open minds to the world without ever having to leave the Ole Mill in Kinsalebeg.

To summer friends Henry sang of the Manchester Rambler before it swept the halls of Ireland. He told the story of our Irish soldiers in the Congo and replaced our tears with laughter when he delivered the fictional tale of the ICA outing which went horribly wrong just when the bachelor brothers had decided their prayers had been answered.

I first met Henry in the 1960s on a magical night in Rooney's of Ardmore. A handsome, broad-shouldered figure with a kind word for everyone and a ballad for every occasion. I saw him another time on the road between Grange and Youghal and we headed to the mill for a night of song and story. For all his banter and twinkling eyes, Henry was a shy man but, like all great artistes, he overcame this when there was an audience to be pleased. For all those who heard him it was more the singer than the song.

Henry loved his pint and he would sit at the counter on the high stool listening with rapt attention to other singers with other stories to tell; the Dutchman who wore wooden shoes and was loved to the end; the accordion player who sang of sweet Aherlow; the man who always claimed we were only passing through as he sang of the town he loved so well. Then Henry would sing of Cavan's gallant John Joe.

Henry died in 1999 and lies beneath Ardmore Tower; no more he'll answer the call: 'sing the one about ...' He lives on in the minds and hearts of those who were lucky enough to have met him on the path of life.

Rest easy Patrick, Luke, Henry and Yehudi.

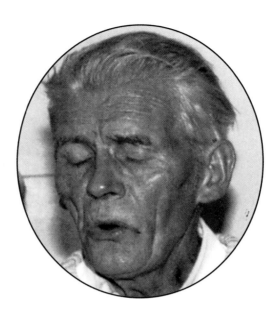

The singer and the song – Henry Curran

Dawn train on the line

The wind had swung south, soon rain would fall on dusty roads, another summer, another year in Ireland was giving up the ghost. It had been a year of highs and lows as each county admitted defeat or went on to the next round only to falter when a McCarthy Cup or Sam Maguire looked to be there for the taking. So much hope, so much disappointment with final joy and success reserved for just two.

So it has gone for a century and more. So it has been for the plain people of Ireland whose Sunday ritual has been early Mass, fried breakfast, prepared sandwiches from batches of hand-sliced bread in brown paper parcels tied with string. Tin foil took over and sealed in the goodness of cooked ham, salad and mayonnaise. There was no forgetting the flask, blue mugs, tea-leaves in envelopes, until they put it in bags and saved the wash-up.

The car, blessed with holy water, a prayer for the safety of all; the priest said the needful for the teams of the day as the clouds broke, the sun smiled down. It was off on the road to Clones, Castlebar, Cork, Tullamore, Kilkenny, or was it, Thurles, Limerick, Killarney or Croke Park?

They say the dawn train from Kerry still travels the line and the talk is of Paddy Bawn and Keohane. Who will ever match the likes of John O', Bomber, Mikey, Pat and Ogie and they winning Sunday after Sunday.

From Cork, into the tunnel and out by Blackpool, it could have been Eudie. Mass on the morning of the great day, maestro Christy Ring striding up from Barry's Hotel to the canal with shouts of: 'Doubt you Ringer boy!' or 'Good on ya, kid' lifting spirits which might light bonfires in Killbarry that evening. It would be four in a row in the 1940s, six medals for Jack, another treble for the Rebels in the 1950s and three again in the 1970s before Teddy Mac would double up in 1990. And there would be glory again in 1999.

Cavan's gallant John Joe and Gunner would see the Polo Grounds in New York and be remembered to this day.

The Dubs would say goodbye to the hill but not before the boys in blue, Paddy, Kevin, Brian and Jimmy, free-taker supreme, would sing it again Sam.

In Kilkenny they talk of Lowry still and Wexford recall the brothers Nicky, Bobby and Billy while the Decies declare they were none to compare with John, Declan, Frankie and Philly.

By Galway's Bay they've had Purcell and Stockwell, the Duggans and Connollys too.

Who will ever forget Tipperary's Tony Reddan in goal, John Doyle and Jimmy's frees from every angle with minutes to play?

Before all that it was Limerick's Mick Mackey who burst the net and turned oppositions green with envy.

Led by Loughnane, Clare would shout from the Burren that we're in the 1990s, the old order changes and that's only fair.

Great minds – Jimmy Barry Murphy and the late Christy Ring

FLIGHT FROM THE LAND

Tom sat on the side of the bed, frozen by the cold and damp of the night, chilled by the thought of what was about to happen. His youngest brother Jim slept soundly in the same bed, his left hand still holding the ragged teddy bear which was no longer the five year old's companion of the day but remained under his pillow to be his comforter by night.

Across the room Tom's other brothers John (17) and Dinny (14) lay on two single beds fitted into the room by the breaking down of a wall to an out-house and bricking up the outer door-way. Tom's sister Mary (19) had the other little room to herself and the parents slept in the gable room across the kitchen. There was a stillness about the cottage as the thatch absorbed the sound of the incessant rain and the only noise came from the neighbour's dog who had caught the scent of a cat or perhaps a rat.

Tom's parents Michael and Mary had met at a platform dance by the cross-roads just a mile away from Michael's own parents' cottage which became his when they died. Mary loved Michael with a fierce passion and those early years of their marriage were to prove the happiest time of her life. Their court-ship was the talk of the area and the gossip reached the ears of the parish priest who was not at all happy that they had been seen walking hand in hand and they not even married.

His mother had told Tom this when he had confided in her that he had been in love with the neighbour's youngest daughter Eileen for over a year and that she was now expecting his child for the following August. Mary told her eldest that she would break the news to Michael at the right time and to leave it to her.

For a few days there was a sort of gloom over the family as father, who had obviously been told by mother of his son's news, kept very much to himself. He was seen walking the lane-ways by the side of the house or going up the hill at the back where his few sheep grazed the short grass between the furze and the rocks.

Then one day they saw Michael talking to Eileen's father where their little plots of land met. After about an hour they were seen to spit on their hands and shake. Michael called the family round him that night. He explained that he and Mary had been thinking for some time that they would like to try and visit his brother and sisters in America. They had been saving for such a trip for over five years and now he felt was the time to do so before they got too old. There was something else which he wanted to tell them. For some years his neighbour had wanted more land to graze his growing dairy herd and Michael was now willing to sell him the three-cornered pasture field on the other side of the hill. The money would go towards the trip to America for the family. And there was something else too. It had been agreed that Tom would be marrying Paddy's Eileen and Michael was handing over the farm to Tom. The newly-weds would be living in the cottage. It was then that the rest of the family knew that the trip to America was not for a holiday but for good.

Tom's sister Mary cried for days at the thought of leaving the place where they had been so happy and the brothers John and Dinny tried to grapple with the thought that they might never see their pals again.

Their father and mother put a brave face on things to take the pressure off Tom who had felt from the beginning that the decision to emigrate had been hastened by his news about his relationship with Eileen. For her part she was heartbroken that her best friend Mary would be leaving but at least she would be her bridesmaid if the parish priest would agree to a full wedding in view of her own news of the baby.

On hearing of the pregnancy the priest delivered a stinging lecture about the lack of morals in society. Then, to her utter surprise, put his arms on her shoulders and said that the ceremony would be in a month's time before she became too obvious. If she was hurt by any gossip she was to come to him and he would deal with it.

Now the wedding day had arrived and the following week his family would be leaving for America. As Tom sat on the bed, he was cheered at the thought of having his own Eileen in his arms and under his roof but he dreaded the thought of seeing his family travel out of their lives – America was after all the other side of the world.

The wedding was a joy and the few days honeymoon in a Cork was blissful. Tom knew that he had made the right choice in Eileen as they stretched against each other, naked and unashamed in the big hotel bed. Their prayer together that previous night had been for their own future happiness, the health of their unborn baby and the success of his family's flight from the land to America.

On the last day of their honeymoon they travelled to Cobh to see off Michael, Mary and their family. They cried as the tender left the quayside to head out the harbour to the waiting liner, the *Titanic*.

The tender all loaded up at Cobh

A passenger watches the docking of a tender with the Titanic

ONE OF THOSE DAYS

It's being cheerful keeps us all going. It was one of those days when it would have been better to turn over, pull up the covers and stay in bed. It's Wednesday, it's wet and dark outside. I thought when I woke that it was Saturday.

The children want to stay in bed and I don't blame them but she who must be obeyed is already in the kitchen, getting their sandwiches ready. I must show example so I fall out of bed, stumble into the bathroom and promise second daughter that I won't be long. I look in the mirror and wonder what happened to the bright young man who would wake singing and look forward to a plate of rashers, sausages and eggs but now could not keep down a bowl of cornflakes.

Car has taken precious children to school, so there is no time even for a cup of tea. My stomach heaves as the bus weaves its way through cold suburbs, windows dripping from condensation. The conductor does not help matters with his 'with feeling' rendering of *Beautiful City*. Place of work is reached and I wonder whatever happened the man on his way to the top who would have a day's work done by now.

It is on such a day that the ESB, P & T, Corporation, County Council and anyone who knows me has sent out missives to fall through the letter-box to lie on the wet floor of the porch. They all announce that the arrears to which they had referred to last month have grown alarmingly. They all suggest that matters will soon be out of their hands if the situation persists. Even the bank managers who look after my many accounts suggest that I might take time out to come up and see them, not sometime, but, now.

Coffee break time comes round and I dash down the street as the rain pours down. My grand entrance through the swinging doors of the bank is spoiled somewhat as I'm pushing the wrong way and the little old lady with the umbrella is not at all happy about her turn on a carousel.

Interview with understanding but firm bank manager is declared a draw and the visiting team heads for street, grateful for at least a point.

Hard day down at the office, I miss the bus, stand in the rain for the next one only to be told it has broken down and another will not be along for another twenty minutes. Home is reached only to find that I have left the meat for the dinner and the paper on the bus. Put my feet up, tell the loved one that I'll watch the news on the telly and she tells me that it's been on the blink ever since youngest and dearest decided that he might be an electrician when he's bigger and fused everything in the sitting-room. Beloved also reminds me that my dinner is still on the bus heading for town.

I spend the evening wondering what kind of mind could set such silly maths questions for youngsters who foolishly think that their dad could answer them. The rain beats down outside and the porch roof leaks. I tell the light of my life that I think I'll have an early night and she mutters something about it must be great to be married to someone who can fix things, run up a kitchen shelf and fix a plug. I try to sleep but the cat on the roof outside the window is in congress with a visiting Persian from up the road.

Then it happens, I wake up. Wednesday has been all a dream and it is Saturday after all. The sun is shining outside. I tap on the floor and I suggest to second youngest that nearest and dearest might send me up a lightly boiled egg and some nice toast with marmalade. Before I can cancel the order I hear heavy breathing and footsteps on the stairs. As bedroom door crashes open I dive for cover.

A SENSE OF HISTORY

My mother had great spirit. Kerry was in her blood, her maternal roots were buried deep in Killorglin. It may have been that Kingdom courage which had her standing up for her beliefs in London when the odds were stacked again a young Irish woman, alone but proud of her origins.

Terence MacSwiney, Lord Mayor of Cork, had died on hunger strike and his remains were to pass through London. My mother Bridie wanted to pay her respects to the patriot as his cortege passed by where my mother was working in government offices. Her manager said she certainly could not have the time off and suggested that if she took it, she would lose her job. My mother stood her ground and I'm sure that the consequences of her actions must have been of deep concern to her. If she was fired, what would she have done. In 1920 there could not have been that many good, pensionable jobs open to Irish girls in a country which had lost so much in the war to end all wars and was still grappling with what would have been euphemistically described as the Irish question. To the credit of her British col-

Sad day in London – remains of Terence MacSwiney are removed

leagues, they supported her plea for time off and she was able to stand on the footpath in silent tribute to a hero and she retained her job.

My mother did return to Ireland and was persuaded by my father, Michael, a handsome, ambitious, hard-working young man to stay at home and marry.

This century, as in every other, people have been central to events or observers of historic times. The changes wrought in these last hundred years could not have been envisaged though Orwell made us all a little nervous coming up to 1984.

They were taking the air by the sea in Bray and Dunlaoghaire when the men of 1916 signalled a desire and determination to be free and paid with their lives.

Michael Collins went to London and brought home the 26 counties but

My mother's hero – Michael Collins

his efforts would lead too to his death as we turned on each other.

We became a nation once again and established the state but international events would overshadow all when Germany invaded Poland and a Second World War looked to engulf the world.

Then Korea and the 38th Parallel would dominate radio news bulletins.

John F. Kennedy would survive the Cold War and the Bay of Pigs but would die from the sniper's bullet in Dallas.

Nixon would pull the Americans out of Vietnam only to sink himself in the Watergate scandal.

This little island would become the focus of the world with the Northern Ireland conflict laying waste whole generations.

First Rhodesia and then South Africa would be sanctioned by the so-called free world and would eventually take their place in the sun.

Man had walked on the moon and looked down on a world which had plenty for some but nothing to offer starving millions. In our time too, Croatia and Kosovo would chill the heart.

Aldous Huxley drew a numbing word picture of a Brave New World and we can only pray that in the new millennium man will heed the lessons of history.

When I look back, I think of the little woman born in Kerry, loved in Cork and realise that sometimes all that is needed for the big world to stay on track is for someone to say: 'This is right and this is what I believe'.

City boy — 2,000 AD

Sullen-brown, storm waters slip by college of all sorts of knowledge; pound their way along the Wessie Bank. Round by the plant of pints, thundering under the South Gate crash the weir before Parliament Bridge as Trinity blesses holy waters mitching from the School of Comm around the corner.

Scampering on to Custom House, after hallowed hall, where freedom of the city is bestowed on Spenser's divided flood as it unionises, waltzes down Marina way to Blackrock Castle which stands up straight, that's why the Rockies can't be bate.

Back in God's own town, houses up and down, in and out, cock a hoop and cock a snoop at cars everywhere, going nowhere.

No parking places but piles of spaces in concrete layers, 1A, 2B or not to be a motorist where tickets lost can land in jail and punch-drunk drivers stick biro through the year, the month, the day, the hour, the minute they parked this way.

In busy streets gum sticks to soles and cobblestones move as shoppers surf windows. Inside glass panes, tailored toy boys and girls stand mute but announce a sale. It's hasta la visa, cheque it out or charge to daddy and have no fear, the tiger prowls, it's been a good year.

Up north, Shandon spirals from Papal Quay where butter mountains rolled long before the EEC. Across the Lee, coal boats stopped where now tented village is bargain-town; come on down, it's Saturday and it's free.

In North Main Street a Vision Centre stands, where once there was prayer but bollards reclaim sacred lands as circumspect motorists mutter and swear blind that footpaths have grown! Could St Francis have known?

St Fin Barre, angels guard thee, as city walls gather round topsy-turvy roofs and abbey ruins remind that Cork was a sacred city long before Liz chartered its course to more modern times when merchant princes looked lovingly down from happy hills.

From Mahon Lough, tunnel vision has linked necklaced roads and roundabouts swirl, islands in the mist, as wheels whirl west, past our childhood fields of dreams. They tell me it's all for the best!

Still waters – a swollen River Lee reflecting City Hall

GLOSSARY

A bob: a shilling coin

All a bah for a sweet: everyone grab a sweet

An Mhaistir: Master, teacher

Annual: once a year book in comic format

Away for slates: everything all right for you

Black and amber: colours of Kilkenny

Blacka jam: blackberry jam

Bóithríns: small roads

Camán: hurley

Capuchin: order of priests

Codded: fooled

Crosser: Crosshaven, seaside village near Cork city

Currach: boat

Donkey's gudge: cake made from baker's left-over ingredients

Eckers: school lessons [homework]

Flake: slap

Flummoxed: greatly surprised

Fond of the jar: likes drink

Gala: swimming races

Grá: love

Halla Deaglán: St Declan's Hall

Howlers: big white lies

Hurl: hurley

ICA: Irish Countrywomen's Association

I'd be beetroot: I'd be embarrassed

Leaba: bed

Líne: row of pupils

Muinteóir: teacher

Pana: Patrick Street

Perks: family owned fun fair

Plamás: flattery

Quarant Ore: forty hours adoration

RIC: Royal Irish Constabulary Force [police]

Rockie: supporter of Blackrock National Hurling Club and/or a native of Blackrock in Cork

Rocky buns: scones with a rough crust

Saigdhiuirí: soldiers [thin slivers of bread]

Swot: student who studies a lot

Tabhair dom do laimhe: give me your hands

Tanora: lemonade drink

Tennis hop: tennis club dance

The Quarry: unofficial playing field on campus [now built upon]

Togs: rugby jersey and pants

Tré Gaeilge: through Irish

V8: type of motor car

Whoppers: lies

Women's Little Christmas: Feast of the Epiphany

ACKNOWLEDGEMENTS

My special thanks are due to the Board of The Examiner Publications and in particular to the Secretary/Director, Anthony Dinan, for generous access to *The Examiner* archives and to the work of its photographers past and present. I am particularly grateful to Lillian Caverley for all her research. I acknowledge also the use of text first published in *The Examiner.*

My sincere thanks to George Mansfield, Regional Director, AIB and to Tina Neylon, Literary Editor, *The Examiner.*

Every effort has been made to establish sources of all photographs used and acknowledgement given – should a source have not been acknowledged, I take this opportunity of apologising for such an oversight and will make the necessary correction at the first opportunity.